THE
SHAAR
PRESS

THE JUDAICA IMPRINT
FOR THOUGHTFUL PEOPLE

LIVING

Published by

Mesorah Publications, ltd

JEWISH

Values, Practices and Traditions

BEREL WEIN

Published by **SHAAR PRESS**
Distributed by MESORAH PUBLICATIONS, LTD.
4401 Second Avenue / Brooklyn, N.Y 11232 / (718) 921-9000

Distributed in Israel by SIFRIATI / A. GITLER
6 Hayarkon Street / Bnei Brak 51127

Distributed in Europe by LEHMANNS
Unit E, Viking Industrial Park, Rolling Mill Road / Jarrow, Tyne and Wear, NE32 3DP/ England

Distributed in Australia and New Zealand by GOLDS WORLD OF JUDAICA
3-13 William Street / Balaclava, Melbourne 3183 / Victoria Australia

Distributed in South Africa by KOLLEL BOOKSHOP
Shop 8A Norwood Hypermarket / Norwood 2196, Johannesburg, South Africa

ISBN: 1-57819-753-8 Hard Cover
ISBN: 1-57819-754-6 Paperback

Printed in the United States of America by Noble Book Press
Custom bound by Sefercraft, Inc. / 4401 Second Avenue / Brooklyn N.Y. 11232

Table of Contents

CHARACTER REFINEMENT

EDUCATION

ESSAYS ON JEWISH HISTORY, THOUGHT AND BELIEFS

Foreword

number of years ago, one of the editors of the *Jerusalem Post* asked me to write a column about Judaism for the paper's weekly International Edition. I agreed to the request and began to write. I called the column "Past Perfect." It dealt with various aspects of Jewish life, ritual, custom and faith, combining both general and specific information. I received a strong response to these columns from Jews and, to my utter surprise, from a large number of non-Jews. Many of my rabbinic colleagues suggested that I write a book based on these columns that would help explain Judaism in a straightforward, uncomplicated manner. I also received a number of requests from non-Jewish clergy to do the same, as they expressed strong interest regarding the people and faith of Israel.

So I redid many of my "Past Perfect" articles, wrote tens of new essays and assembled the material into this book that you are now reading. I have named the book

Living Jewish, since that is exactly what the book describes. What does a Jew believe? How is a Jew to behave? What are the highlights of the Jewish calendar and why is the Sabbath so important? What is the Jew's relationship to the Land and State of Israel? The book deals with these and many other issues. It is not a polemic, nor an apology. It is simply a recounting of the facts about Judaism, as I know them. I hope that all readers will therefore benefit from this work.

My deep appreciation goes to Charlotte Friedland for her keen editorial eye and her insight and suggestions. Shaar Press/Mesorah Publications has been my sole publisher for my other books and I appreciate their efforts in publishing and presenting this one as well. My thanks go to my wife and family for their forbearance and encouragement while I was writing this book. A frustrated author hitting a moment of writer's block is not easy to deal with, especially when you need his help in the house. My wife is a master at soothing that beast.

I pray to the God of Israel, Who has sustained me in life and health and allowed me to dwell in His holy city, that my words find favor in His eyes and in the eyes of humans as well. And I sincerely hope that this book will contribute to a better and more favorable attitude towards Judaism, its customs, values and adherents.

Berel Wein
Jerusalem, Israel
Tishrei 5763/September 2002

Life Cycle Events

*A*ll life cycle events are marked by Jewish ritual law, custom and tradition. These elements give the event deeper meaning, eternal memory and spiritual content, instead of merely being viewed as occurrences that are natural and normal in the life span of a human being.

In Jewish life, every occurrence in personal and family life has a meaning far more intense than the event itself. All personal things in Jewish life also influence the entire Jewish People, and eventually the entire world. They have cosmic consequences of which we ordinary humans are not necessarily always aware. This is why life cycle events are commemorated in Judaism in a religious fashion — so that they are not merely a notice of a passage of time and the constant change of generations.

Judaism does not recognize any "ordinary" events in one's life cycle. Since all of these events are extraordinary, they deserve extraordinary methods of remembrance and commemoration. They underscore the realization that life is relatively short and always fleeting. This section of the book deals with many life cycle events and how Jewish laws and traditions enrich each experience.

1 Birth

n the eyes of Jewish tradition, the birth of a child is always a joyous and momentous event. The Biblical injunction "to be fruitful and settle the world" is a cornerstone of Jewish belief. The general rule of welcoming children into the world and seeing in children a blessing, and not merely a burden and responsibility (which they certainly are also!), is deeply rooted in Jewish practice and in the Jewish psyche.

The birth of a Jewish baby is both a personal satisfaction and a national joy. This certainly is so currently because there are very few Jews in the world, relatively speaking. In a world of over six billion human beings, there are barely 14 million of them who identify themselves as being Jewish. The demographic tragedy of the Jewish People is very stark. In 1939, there were 19 million Jews in the world. More than 60 years later, according to the statistics of natural increase, there should be over 50 million Jews in the world. What happened to the more than 36 million missing Jews? The Holocaust, assimilation, intermarriage and a very low birthrate among many Jewish families provide most of the answers to this heartrending question. Thus, simply because there are so few of us, every Jewish child that is born is to be regarded as the treasure that it truly is.

But the joy goes deeper than that. When friends and relatives say, "Mazal tov!" when seeing a newborn, they are expressing their happiness that another Jew has been added to the world — a Jew who will ultimately serve as a link from generations of the past to generations of the future. Inherent in that link are thousands of years of traditions, beliefs, and practices, and a sense of humanity that Jews know it is their mission and privilege to carry.

Because children are the carriers of our national destiny, midwifery was a widely accepted and honorable role in Jewish life. According to Jewish tradition, the mother of Moses, as well as his sister, were the leaders and teachers of the Jewish midwives in Egypt towards the end of the period of Jewish enslavement there. They lived at a time of unexpected and unexplained explosive growth of the Jewish population then in Egypt. They were the ones who refused Pharaoh's order to butcher all Jewish males at birth, despite the fact that it could have cost them their own lives. Thus the midwife entered the Jewish story as a heroine, a role that she retained for centuries.

Today that honor has devolved to the doctor, midwife and birthing coach — in fact, everyone who helps to bring a new life into the world. The process of birth is regarded by Jewish tradition as a time of danger for both mother and child. Special prayers and Psalms are recited by friends and family when the mother-to-be is in labor, in order to ease the labor process and prepare the way for the birth of a healthy and normal child. Many of the restrictions of Jewish law are suspended regarding a woman in labor and for a period of time after she has given birth.

The life of the mother has primacy over that of her fetus and only when the baby is actually born does the *halachah* (Jewish law) equate it with the life of the mother. Nevertheless, the general rule in Jewish law is that a fetus is not to be aborted unless the mother's life is threatened by it. This is because the fetus is regarded as a separate entity with a body and soul of its own, not merely as part of its mother's body, for most legal matters. The question of abortion is a most complex Jewish legal issue and expert rabbinical opinion is required in all individual instances. But the general public policy of traditional Judaism was and is against abortion, certainly against abortion on demand, when there are no legal reasons present to allow it.

Once the baby has been born, its first Sabbath is a special one. Daughters are officially named during the Torah-reading in the synagogue, which takes place on Mondays, Thursdays and the Sabbath. In addition to proclaiming her name, parents (and often, grandparents) customarily sponsor a *Kiddush* — refreshments for the entire congregation after the services — to publicly express their joy over the birth of their daughter.

For baby boys, the first Sabbath has special significance as well. Since the circumcision is never done before the eighth day of a boy's life, there is automatically a Sabbath in that child's life before the ceremony takes place. A Friday evening reception called *Shalom Zachor* is held in honor of the newborn son in the home of the parents or at the synagogue, and friends and neighbors come to extend their blessings.

With or without such receptions, the birth of a child is always a special and signal event in family life. Because the Jewish People views itself as one large family, the birth of every Jewish child is an important occasion for all of the Children of Israel.

The Covenant
of Abraham: Brit

2

The tradition of Judaism, thousands of years old, is to circumcise its male children on the eighth day after their birth. This act of ritual circumcision is based on the narrative in the Bible in which the Lord tells Abraham that this act of circumcision is to be the immutable sign of His covenant between Abraham and his descendants for all time. Abraham's son, Ishmael, is circumcised at the age of thirteen, according to the Biblical narrative. This is the basis for male circumcision at that age in the Moslem world. However, Isaac, the son of Abraham and Sarah, was circumcised on the eighth day of his life and this became Jewish practice throughout the ages. Naturally, if the infant is deemed physically unable to safely withstand the procedure on the eighth day of his life, the circumcision is postponed until such time that it can be safely performed. If the boy is healthy, the circumcision is performed on the eighth day, even if that eighth day falls on the Sabbath or one of the Jewish holidays, days when such "work" is ordinarily forbidden.

Jews have always sacrificed much, even their lives, to perpetuate and perform this defining act of Jewishness. The covenant of Abraham gives this ceremony its name — brit, the Hebrew word for a covenant. The brit is mentioned in the daily blessings recited after eating as being "the covenant with the Lord that has been sealed in our flesh." The prophet Ezekiel proclaimed that Israel would live eternally, as the blood of circumcision bespeaks the readiness for self-sacrifice that exists eternally within the Jewish People.

The actual surgery consists of three stages: the removal of the foreskin with a special surgical knife; the reshaping of the organ without the foreskin; and the guarantee of normal blood circulation in the affected area by the drawing of some blood before the area is bandaged and the blood flow staunched. The surgery itself is traditionally performed by a mohel — a ritual circumciser who is a specialist in this medical procedure and in the Jewish laws governing it.

The ceremony usually takes place in the home of the infant or in the family's synagogue, and is a most festive occasion. Blessings are recited over a cup of wine and the baby is then and there given his Jewish name. (Girls are named in the synagogue at the Torah reading on the first Sabbath of their lives.) The congregation and guests present at the circumcision ceremony say in unison the Hebrew blessing that "just as the boy has entered into the Covenant of Abraham, so too may he grow up healthy and well and enter Bar Mitzvah, the wedding canopy and the continued accomplishments of a life of good deeds."

A meal is served to all present, with words of Torah thought and family nostalgia delivered between the courses of food being served. Sometimes this can make for a long meal. Almost always, though, it is an emotional occasion, no matter what the duration of the meal may be.

There are many different honors that are distributed to members of the family, friends or dignitaries present during the circumcision ceremony. These include bringing the baby into the room for the ceremony, holding the baby while the blessings are recited, holding the baby while he is receiving his name, naming the baby, reciting the blessings, and carrying the baby out of the room at the conclusion of the ceremony.

The primary honor is given to the *sandak*, who holds the baby on his lap when the surgery is being performed. This honor is usually given to a grandfather or some other distinguished personage. Since Jewish tradition teaches us that the Prophet Elijah is present at all circumcisions, to bear witness to Jewish loyalty to its covenant with God, a special chair is prepared for Elijah. The baby is placed on that chair before being lifted and given to the *sandak* for the circumcision. Many synagogues have an ornate "Elijah's chair" for use at circumcision ceremonies. Thus, the circumcision ceremony is an emotional combination of tradition, mysticism, surgical precision, family pride and joy — and is the ultimate expression of Jewish commitment to its past and its future destiny.

Redeeming the Firstborn Son: Pidyon HaBen

3

One of the most emotional and colorful ceremonies celebrated in Jewish life is that of the *Pidyon HaBen* — the process of "redeeming" the firstborn son. This ceremony occurs on the thirty-first day of the infant boy's life (but not on Sabbath or holidays), and often in the late afternoon. The ceremony itself is customarily followed by an elaborate meal that may include toasts and speeches in honor of the baby and his family.

There are three basic requirements necessary for the ceremony:

A mother's firstborn healthy baby boy;

A Kohen — a member of the priestly clan of Jews, descended from Aharon, the first High Priest of Israel;

Five coins of pure, or almost pure, silver.

The purity of the silver coins deemed acceptable for the ceremony varies from 88% to 96%. There was a time when old American silver dollars were in vogue as the coin of choice. However, the modern American silver dollars contain far too much dross to be used. Even the old American silver dollars usually required six coins in order to equal the proper amount. Much in vogue today are silver coins specially minted by the Israeli government, expressly for use at a *Pidyon HaBen*. These coins have a high silver content (96%) and are beautiful in form and design. The five coins are purchased or acquired by the father of the baby boy before the ceremony and are given by him to the Kohen as the means of redeeming the child. It is the silver content of the coins that is important and not their country of origin.

What do we mean by "redeem" in this instance? The Torah states that the firstborn Israelites were "redeemed" — i.e. exempt — by God from the plague that killed the firstborn Egyptians. This blow, the last of the Ten Plagues, finally cracked Pharaoh's will and he allowed the Jewish slaves to leave Egyptian bondage. (Because the plague struck only male Egyptians, only Jewish males owed their lives to God's special attention.) The firstborn Jewish males were thereafter considered consecrated to God's service. They later involuntarily forfeited this honor when they participated in the building of the Golden Calf in the Sinai desert. In their stead, the tribe of Levi, which refused to participate in the Golden Calf debacle, and specifically the priestly family of Aaron, were thereafter consecrated to perform the holy services in the Temple. Thus firstborn males of Kohanim and of the tribe of Levi are exempted from the requirement of the *Pidyon HaBen* ceremony.

The Torah enjoined the remaining Jews to redeem their firstborn sons from the priest/Kohen after the child passed through his first month of life. The ceremony underscores the recognition that children are gifts to their parents from God and that the Lord holds them responsible to His service. This dedication of the child to a noble Jewish life, which this ceremony implies, becomes the central theme in the raising and educating of all Jewish children, even those who are not firstborn.

The infant is usually brought into the room for the ceremony on a silver tray. There is a custom that the women present at the ceremony place pieces of their own jewelry on that tray as a symbol that human life — a child — is worth far more than all of the wealth of this world. (They do receive their jewelry back when the ceremony is concluded!) The father and the Kohen recite the blessings for the *Pidyon HaBen*, the coins are given to the Kohen, and he then blesses the child with the priestly blessing. The participants (except the baby) drink from a cup of wine over which blessings have been recited. A festive family meal follows, with the good wishes of all.

As every parent knows, the five silver coins are only the beginning of the lifetime investment the parents will make for the welfare of their child.

4 Bat Mitzvah

n recognition of the earlier age of physical, emotional and social maturity arrived at by women compared to men, the age of Bat Mitzvah established by Jewish tradition is twelve, instead of the thirteen years for the Bar Mitzvah of young men. As the name Bat Mitzvah implies — literally "a daughter of obligation" — girls at age twelve become responsible in regard to the ritual requirements of Jewish life. It is both an obligation and a privilege to keep God's laws. When the young woman has previously achieved knowledge and training in these ritual requirements during her childhood, the transition to becoming a Bat Mitzvah is usually smooth and seamless.

Bat Mitzvah celebrations and commemorations have undergone many societal changes throughout Jewish history. Only the fact of Bat Mitzvah itself and its marking of the coming of age and responsibility of Jewish women has remained constant throughout time.

For many centuries of Jewish life, both in the Sephardic and Ashkenazic communities, the Bat Mitzvah celebration for a Jewish girl remained a private, family-oriented event. Perhaps there was a dinner held at home, and the girl received the blessings of her family. In the main, this form of celebration was true of her brother's Bar Mitzvah as well. For boys, no special festivity ensued at the age of thirteen, except for the fact that the young man was called to receive an honor at the Torah reading of the week. Over the past century, the Bar Mitzvah party for boys has become much more public, elaborate and expensive. Over the past decades, this has become true for Bat Mitzvah celebrations as well.

The expansion of the Bat Mitzvah ceremony also parallels the changing role and new intensive forms of Jewish education for women. It is quite common today — but by no means required — for the young woman to deliver a talk about a Torah subject at her Bat Mitzvah celebration. Where this talk is given differs with custom within various Jewish communities. Many times, the talk is devoted to the lessons of life derived from the great Jewish heroines and personalities of the Bible and Talmud. Miriam, Esther, Ruth and Bruriah (the scholarly wife of Rabbi Meir of Talmudic fame) are often chosen as the centerpieces of Bat Mitzvah discourses. As women's education has become more and more sophisticated, the Bat Mitzvah's presentation may be quite impressive in content, style and scholarship.

Some Jewish societies have the custom of introducing a woman to the commandment of lighting Sabbath candles when she attains the age of Bat Mitzvah. In other communities, the obligation of performing this holy act of sanctification, which brings the blessings of the Sabbath into the Jewish home, is postponed until marriage. Many young girls also begin at Bat Mitzvah age to take instruction in baking *challah*, the special bread of Sabbath, which is associated with the commandment of removing a tithe of dough from the dough before baking. It is interesting to note that the Hebrew name of the bread is taken from the commandment involved in its preparation: *Challah* is literally the piece of dough removed before baking. Though in our current

Jewish world women do not look to their kitchens as their life's endeavor, the baking of *challah* remains a cherished task for many Jewish women. It is eagerly pursued by thousands of young women reaching the age of Bat Mitzvah. (And if you've ever eaten a fresh-baked *challah*, you will agree that this is a tradition that should never be lost.)

As with Bar Mitzvah, it is often the private ritual performed with enthusiasm and joy in one's home that marks the true spirit of becoming Bat Mitzvah more than the public scholarly performance and party. The knowledge that one is now a part of the Jewish nation in full standing imparts a sense of honor and belonging coupled with a mature acceptance of responsibility. There is no greater teacher of adult accountability and dignity than the Bar or Bat Mitzvah celebrated with meaningful priorities.

5 Bar Mitzvah

The time of Bar Mitzvah is when a young man reaches the age of thirteen years and one day. This is based upon the halachic (Jewish legal) presumption that this is certainly the time of the onset of puberty in males. The Talmud discusses becoming a Bar Mitzvah less in terms of achieving a certain age and more in terms of visible body signs of puberty. Nevertheless, it has become commonly accepted practice to grant the halachic status of "manhood" to young men on the day after their thirteenth birthday without scrutiny as to their actual physical pubescence.

On the day of Bar Mitzvah, a Jewish young man joins the timeless ranks of the People of Israel and becomes legally obligated to fulfill the commandments of the Torah. He is included in the congregation of Israel for such privileges as being counted as part of a *minyan* (a necessary quorum of ten males) for prayer and for the special Grace After Meals, among other rituals. But these privileges and obligations are somewhat technical compared to the fact that the young man is now expected to embrace the value system and lifestyle hallowed by Jewish families for millennia. This is a lifelong task and goal. Although thirteen is a rather tender age to impose such serious business on boys, the truth is that, for many people, adolescence forms us for life: A Jewish lifestyle begun at the beginning of that formative and potentially dangerous stage of life is the surest guarantee of reaching adult maturity with Jewish knowledge, tradition and values as part of one's makeup.

In truth, thirteen was not such a young age in the earlier stages of human civilization. Life expectancy was much shorter than it is today and children stopped being children at about the age of nine. It was not uncommon in the Jewish world, both in the Middle East and in Eastern Europe, for couples to be married at the age of thirteen! This social practice gave rise to the wry quip of a great rabbi who was faced with the problem of having a *chattan* (bridegroom) and a Bar Mitzvah boy in the synagogue on the very same Sabbath. The question arose as to which one of them had precedence in receiving the honor to read from the Torah. The wise rabbi responded: "Whoever is older!"

Bar Mitzvah celebrations in today's Jewish world are quite elaborate, if not even grossly overdone. In previous generations, when few Jews could ever hope to be considered affluent, Bar Mitzvah boys were called to the Torah, but not necessarily on Shabbat; he could be called on a Monday or Thursday during the week, when the Torah was read publicly during the morning service. A piece of cake, salted herring and a good shot of whisky were the menu for the celebratory Bar Mitzvah "banquet" following the service. Obviously, many "themed" Bar Mitzvah celebrations today, which have little Jewish content, are inconsistent with the idea of Bar Mitzvah itself.

It is customary for the Bar Mitzvah boy to speak at the celebration. Words of Torah, of appreciation to parents and teachers and of commitment to a Jewish future make up the traditional Bar Mitzvah speech. Traditionally the boy's grandparents purchased the *tefillin* (phylacteries) for him. (He would use them for morning prayers for the rest of his life.) From that custom arose the practice of relatives and friends presenting the Bar Mitzvah boy with other gifts, and this latter custom is "religiously" adhered to throughout the Jewish world today.

The milestone of Bar Mitzvah is appreciated usually only much later in life. I have often remarked, only half-facetiously, that if it were up to me, Bar Mitzvah should be postponed till age forty-three. Then the full impact of life as a Jew and as an adult would be present.

Be that as it may, we will rejoice with our thirteen-year-olds as they enter the ranks of the Eternal People and hold back our tears of joy. As a grandparent who recently attended the Bar Mitzvah of his grandson, I can attest that thirteen-year-old boys do not appreciate weeping grandparents!

6 The Wedding

By its very nature, a Jewish wedding ceremony can be described as being simple and joyous. It is composed of four sections. The first consists of the recital of the two blessings of *eyrusin* — the blessings that pledge the couple to each other to the exclusion of all others — and their drinking from the same cup of wine. However, these blessings do not yet allow the couple to live together as husband and wife. That only occurs at the end of the entire ceremony. The second part of the ceremony consists of the groom placing the ring on the right index finger of the bride. As he does so, he pronounces the time-honored vow of Jewish family life: "You are hereby sanctified to me according to the laws of Moses and Israel."

Aside from the spiritual, physical and emotional bond that the wedding ceremony creates between the bride and groom, there is also a legal aspect. The placing of the ring on the bride's finger in front of accredited and worthy witnesses is the legal act of the marriage in Jewish law.

Without such legality occurring, the other aspects of the marriage are hollow, even illegal, under Jewish law and tradition. The ring must be plain, without any precious stones, but its simple circle of metal symbolizes the cycle of life and pure holiness that Torah represents for us.

The third segment of the wedding ceremony among Ashkenazic Jews is the reading of the *ketubah,* the document stating the legal, monetary and physical undertakings of a Jewish husband towards his wife. The Ashkenazim usually insert a standard sum as the actual minimum monetary value of the undertaking. Sephardim usually insert a different sum for each couple being married, that sum many times becoming the subject of intense negotiation between the families of the bride and groom. As such, the Sephardim rarely read the *ketubah* out loud and substitute for it words of blessing by the performing rabbi. Ashkenazim may also have the rabbi speak to the bride and groom, though that is an option and not a necessary portion of the ceremony.

After the reading of the *ketubah,* the document is handed by the groom to his bride, again under the watchful eyes of witnesses. It is hers for the rest of their lives together. Lately, the ancient custom of having personalized, artistic, illuminated *ketubah* documents used for this ceremony has been renewed, much to the delight of Jewish artists and calligraphers. (Often the *ketubah* is framed and displayed in the couple's home.)

The final section of the wedding ceremony consists of the recitation of the *Sheva Brachot* — the *birchot nisuim* — the blessings that actually declare the bride and groom to be now husband and wife in Jewish law and tradition. These blessings describe the joy of family and the love of husband and wife for each other; they thank God for creation, for life itself, for the joy of marriage and for the eventual complete redemption of Zion and Israel. They present the challenge of marriage and its blessings, and of the faith and love necessary to sustain a family and a stable marriage. After these blessings have been recited, a glass is broken to signify that our happiness is yet incomplete because of the loss of the Temple of Jerusalem.

And then the joy erupts. Celebrating with the bride and groom is one of the great traditions of the Jewish People. Dancing, singing, performing juggling and clown acts, as well as other forms of entertainment are all part of the wedding celebration. In Eastern Europe, a special comedian/entertainer — a *badchan* — was engaged to entertain the audience with recitations of stories, both hilarious and sad, special poems customized to the particular bride and groom and their families, and with original and melodious song. The art of the multi-talented *badchan* has not been completely lost; they can still be found at some very traditional weddings. Accompanied by instrumental music, the celebrations usually last well into the night. Simplicity and joy represents the Jewish wedding. It also represents the Jewish family and home at its best.

Death in
Jewish Tradition

7

The subject of death has fascinated humans from the beginning of time. Both the philosophy and physiology of death have been dealt with in innumerable works, studies and theories. I am not equipped to discuss the mysteries of death, but I do wish to discuss the Jewish attitude and the view of Jewish law in the instance of death.

Approximately 200,000 Jews attended the funeral of the great Rabbi Elazar Menachem Mann Shach in Israel (in 2002). They exemplify the idea of *levayah,* literally accompaniment of the deceased to his final resting place. *Levayah,* therefore, is the Hebrew term for funeral, yet the focus is on the living beings performing this important *mitzvah,* which is both a commandment and tradition of the Jews. It is, in fact, one of the actions that the rabbis of the Talmud say "is rewarded in this world and remain as a merit for the World to Come." Attending a funeral is inconvenient. It interrupts our daily schedule and never is a planned or especially pleasant event. Yet, since mortality is the lot of all humans, Jewish tradition pre-scribes how to deal with it.

Giving proper final respect to the deceased is seen as a holy obligation. That burial of the dead is an obligation derived from the Torah commandment to "imitate" our Creator, so to speak. The Torah records that, "… He buried him (Moses) there in the valley." "He" refers to the Lord Himself. Because God prepared Moses for burial and buried him Himself, we "imitate" God in fulfilling our obligation to bury our dead, and we accord the deceased the respect of being accompanied by one's fellow mortals on the final journey of this earthly existence. In every Jewish community there exists a purely voluntary *chevra kadisha* — literally, holy society — that cleanses and washes the body of the deceased and dresses it in white shrouds for proper Jewish burial.

This concept of "imitating" God is central to all Jewish social values and commandments, implying that we are meant to be godly beings, using our abilities to benefit others. It is the basis for the commandments of attending and visiting the sick, helping the poor and defenseless, rejoicing at weddings and other staples of Jewish communal life. The attributes of God that are described in the Torah are not meant so much to explain God to us — an impossibility in any instance — but to instruct us as to how and in what ways humans can emulate the attributes of the Creator.

At about the same time of the death of Rabbi Shach, the Israeli Defense Forces and its Chief Rabbi declared three soldiers who had been kidnapped by the Hezbollah terrorists in 2001 as dead, even though the whereabouts of their corpses are unknown. The parents and families of the two Jewish soldiers, after consulting with the Chief Rabbi of the IDF, began their period of mourning. Even though there is some sense of closure that this period of mourning will bring to the distraught families, the lack of bodies to bury or a grave to visit will prevent the complete closure that the observance of Jewish ritual mourning intends to accomplish.

The observance of the traditional Jewish ritual of the seven days of "sitting *shiva*," and later thirty days of mourning, during which friends visit to comfort and express empathy and sympathy, certainly aids the families in coping with their loss. Curtailing the mourning period is actually a disservice to the mourners, who Jewish tradition recognizes are in need of this transitional period before returning to the normal routines of their lives.

Judaism is a religion of life that does not glorify death. We have no room for suicide bombers or gratuitous murderers in the Jewish worldview. The Torah bids us to "choose life" and that is where the emphasis lies in Jewish existence. While Judaism does not dwell upon the subject of death, Jewish law addresses the reality of death head on, without the euphemisms and avoidance of reality about it that is prevalent in the Western culture surrounding us. It is in the ritual observance of the commandments and traditions, the customs and accepted behavior of Jews over the centuries, that death finds its proper place in the framework of life itself.

The Funeral:
8 Saying Good-bye

espite the modern bravado of calling funerals "a celebration of life," it is obvious to all that funerals are very depressing affairs. In most instances, death is an unwelcome event, if not always to the deceased person, certainly almost always to the family and friends of the deceased. The tendency in the Western world is to somehow mask death, to pretty it up and to make funerals sterile, hushed, overly courteous and somewhat surrealistic events.

Not so in Jewish tradition and understanding. In the Bible, we read that Jewish society in Biblical times employed professional mourners and weepers to raise the emotions of the participants at a funeral, to bring them to tears as well. These professional mourners were usually women and this profession was deemed an honorable and necessary service to Jewish society. This is because emotional outpourings of grief are deemed acceptable, if not even necessary, at Jewish funerals. Of course, there are funerals where the circumstances are so tragic that emotional grief needs no encouragement. But even at "normal" funerals, for people who lived long and fruitful lives, expressions of grief are acceptable and warranted. The Hebrew word for funeral is *levayah*, which means accompaniment. The deceased goes to his or her eternal reward "accompanied" by those who were friends in life (and accompanied as well by his or her own good deeds). No one goes alone.

The funeral service in Jewish tradition includes the recitation of appropriate chapters from the Bible, usually from the Book of Psalms. Though some of the Biblical readings recited are almost standard at all funerals — such as the twenty-third psalm of David ("The Lord is my shepherd...") or the final chapter of Proverbs ("A woman of valor...) — the exact Biblical readings may be adjusted to express the life and character of the deceased. Eulogies are always part of the funeral service, except during time periods (holidays, the month of Nissan, etc.) when eulogies are not offered because they would interfere with the required joyous mood of the day.

The eulogy is also meant to raise the emotions of those assembled for the funeral. The Talmud mentions that the soul of the deceased is aware of the eulogy. For this reason, canned, one-size-fits-all eulogies are inappropriate. Traditionally, the eulogy was delivered by the rabbi of the community or by another notable. Also, there were professional eulogizers in Jewish society, almost always men, who paralleled the effect of the professional women mourners in eliciting emotional expressions of grief from those assembled at the funeral. The Talmud is strict in mandating that the exact truth be told in assessing other human beings while they were still alive. However, as far as eulogies were concerned, this rule was relaxed, allowing for slight exaggeration of the deceased's good qualities and the omission of references to any of his or her unpleasant qualities and/or deeds. In any event, good judgment and a great deal of intuitive sensitivity towards the feelings of the mourners, the reputation of the deceased and that of the family, the assembled audience and the community generally, is always necessary in measuring one's words when delivering a eulogy.

Over the past few decades, a trend has developed in which children and grandchildren deliver the eulogies. Traditionally, this was almost never the case, with the eulogies almost always delivered by outsiders rather than the family members themselves. However, this new custom of immediate family members delivering the eulogy is widely accepted today. After the eulogy is completed, the memorial prayer for the deceased ("*Kayl Malay Rachamim...*") is intoned, often sung by a cantor. *Kaddish* is recited and the body is taken to the cemetery for interment.

Jewish tradition teaches that the deceased be buried wearing a simple white shroud. The shrouds are the same for all, rich and poor, leader and unknown citizen, the scholarly and the unlettered. As King Solomon stated, "There is no station in life left on the day of death." Tradition also informs us that the deceased should be buried in a simple wood coffin. In Israel, as well as in many other Jewish communities in the world, even this wooden coffin is dispensed with and the body is laid to rest in the grave in its shrouds alone.

There are voluntary burial societies in nearly every Jewish community. They are called *chevra kadisha* (holy society). This group cleans and washes the body, dresses it in its shrouds and prepares it for dignified burial. (A male *chevra kadisha* performs this service for men; women take care of deceased females.) These societies are not-for-payment organizations and are the mechanism for fair, equal, holy and dignified treatment of all Jewish deceased, no matter what affiliations or non-affiliation the person had in life. It is deemed the highest form of altruism and Jewish kindness to be a member of such a society and participate in its work.

Jewish law also prescribes the rending of the outer garment of the deceased's near relatives, as a sign of their grief and mourning. There is a cathartic benefit to the expression of grief by behavior and emotion. Judaism recognized that cathartic expression. The tearing of only a black ribbon is not in consonance with

Jewish tradition and usually fails to give the mourner the maximum cathartic benefit needed to eventually recover from grief.

At the cemetery, Psalms are again recited and the body is lowered into the grave. After the grave is filled with earth, a reading of the appropriate verses acknowledging God's immortality and man's mortality (and thus our acceptance of God's will and perfect, infinite judgment) is delivered. This is again followed by the recitation of the *Kaddish*. The immediate family then leaves the cemetery, walking between two rows of those assembled, who bless them with the traditional Jewish prayer of comfort: "May the Almighty comfort you among those who mourn the destruction of Zion and Jerusalem." The catharsis of grief and the acknowledgment of death, which are the bases of the Jewish funeral service, also form the bases for the restructuring of the lives of the mourners and their passage into more joyous times.

The Annual Yahrzeit:
9 Memorial Days

Yahrzeit is a *Yiddish* word that literally means "time of year," but traditionally has always been expanded to mean the anniversary of the date of death of close relatives or well-known personages in Jewish history. The Sephardim and other non-*Yiddish* speaking Jews call the day *yom zikaron* — day of remembrance. The Talmud does not mention *yahrzeit* per se, except for a reference that it was customary to fast on the anniversary of the death date of a parent. But the observance of *yahrzeit* took on added importance and ritual content as the centuries passed. Because of the understandably enormous emotional hold that it had on people, *yahrzeit* became an intensely observed custom throughout the Jewish world. The recent community-wide observance of *Yom Hashoah* is an example of a mass *yahrzeit* observance for the six million Jews killed in the Holocaust.

It is customary to light a candle that will burn for twenty-four hours at the eve of the day of *yahrzeit*. The symbolism of the candle is taken from a verse in Proverbs — "God's candle is the human soul." The rabbis of *Midrash* stated that this verse is the companion piece to the verse: "...God's commandments are as a candle and the Torah is light." The *Midrash* concludes, therefore, that God tells us, so to speak: "My candle — the Torah — is in your hands; and your candle — the soul — is in My hands. If you will guard My candle from being extinguished, I will guard your candle from being extinguished. But if you will neglect My candle, then your candle will also flicker and go out." By lighting a candle on the *yahrzeit* of a dear deceased relative, we proclaim our faith in the covenant that these two verses imply.

The day of *yahrzeit* is also commemorated by the recitation of the Mourner's *Kaddish* at the synagogue services on that day. In addition, the person marking the *yahrzeit* for his parents is accorded priority in leading the synagogue services. This is in accordance with the understanding that the leader of the services has a special merit in so doing, since he "causes" the congregation to bless God's name. This merit accrues to the memory of the soul of the deceased whose *yahrzeit* is being observed that day. In addition, it is customary for the one observing the *yahrzeit* to be called to the Torah reading on the Sabbath preceding the *yahrzeit*. In many congregations, the one observing *yahrzeit* is called for the *maftir* reading (the concluding portion of the Sabbath Torah reading, including the recitation of the appropriate reading from the Prophets for that Sabbath.) All of this is also done in order to allow the one observing *yahrzeit* to gain the merit of the response of the congregation to the blessing of God's name, which the blessings of the Torah and *haftorah* occasion.

Many people also use the occasion of *yahrzeit* to visit the grave of the deceased and there offer memorial prayers on behalf of that person's soul. Judaism is not a religion of death and graves. It celebrates life and places far greater emphasis on living as a Jew than dying as one. Yet since the death of a beloved relative is always a traumatic experience and leaves a permanent scar on one's psyche, observance of *yahrzeit* and its attendant customs assuages grief and gives solace to those who yet feel pained by the loss of loved ones. Perhaps that is why *yahrzeit* has been one of the most cherished and widely observed customs in Jewish traditional life.

10 **Immortality**

ore potent than the apprehension of death itself is the apprehension of what lies after life in this world. One of the basic principles of Judaism is that there is an afterlife beyond death — known in Jewish lore as the "World to Come." The principle of afterlife is not directly mentioned in the exact wording of the verses of the Bible, though it is alluded to in many places in the Biblical texts. The Jewish principles of responsibility for one's behavior, for freedom of choice, justice and the corollary concept of reward and punishment presuppose an afterlife where reward for good and punishment of evil can be meted out.

The return of the soul to the Creator who fashioned it and placed it in a human body is the Jewish concept of death. The soul, that Godly part of us, survives the physical death of the body. It is judged in the afterlife on the basis of its performance on earth in this life. It is rewarded for its good deeds and punished for its wrongdoings.

The soul then lives on in the eternal world that is associated with God's spirit in the World to Come. How that soul lives in the world of the spirit, and under what conditions, is within the framework of reward and punishment.

Even those souls that are punished for their wrongdoings do not necessarily have an eternal sentence of punishment and rejection. Talmudic tradition is that these malefactors are punished for a twelve-month period, after which their cleansed souls are restored to Divine acceptance. There is a tradition that the acts of children in this world can help ameliorate the suffering of their parents' (and other relatives') souls in the World to Come. The *Kaddish* prayer, recited by mourners in the synagogue during the first year after the passing of parents and other loved ones, is one of the means of accomplishing that purpose.

On what criteria is the soul judged? The rabbis of the Talmud declare that the three main issues dealt with in the judgment of the soul in the afterlife are:

1) Study, observance and support of Torah

2) Honesty and integrity in dealing with other human beings

3) Maintaining the expectation that the Jewish People and all mankind will someday enter the Messianic era in which knowledge of God and obedience to His will would be normal, accepted features of daily life.

In a general way, one can say that almost all details of everyday life in this world of mortal existence fit into one of these three categories. In reality, all Jewish values and lifestyle are expressed in the challenges posed by those three categories of eternal judgment. Life in this world, therefore, should be lived in accordance with how those issues will be raised in the World to Come. In that world — also known as the "World of Truth" — the soul will no longer be able to rationalize wrongdoing, but will have to openly admit the truth in answer to every question about its life on earth.

Another aspect of immortality is how we will be remembered by later generations. There is an inner craving within all of us to be remembered, to be immortal. History, even private family lore, has the last vote about people, their ideas, actions and contributions to society. How will our grandchildren remember and appreciate us? That is an important question in Jewish life. My mentors in my yeshivah days taught us that a Jewish life is to be lived in such a fashion that both our grandparents and our grandchildren will be proud of us. What we leave behind in spirit and inspiration, good memories and pious deeds, will far outlive whatever material benefits, no matter how extravagant, that we will leave behind for our offspring.

Immortality is thus earned daily, in the everyday activities of life in this world. In fact, it is through family, students, friends, associates, scholarship, proper action and benevolent deeds that we slowly forge the stuff of true immortality in this world, as well as in the World to Come."

Family Life

*J*ewish society — in fact, Jewish faith and practice — rests on the institution of the family. The Jewish home always has been seen as the bastion of Jewish survival and as the most essential component of Jewish living. Torah, tradition, customs, attitudes and Weltanschauung are taught within the secure confines of the Jewish family. Schools are important in Jewish society, but families are always more important. Family life is meant to exhibit the omnipresence of God in one's life and home. God is truly a member of the Jewish household and He has a voice, via Jewish law and lore, in all family matters.

The Jewish People sees itself not only as a nation or as a religion, but most importantly as a family. There is a relationship of kinship among Jews that binds us all together, no matter how diverse we are in character, outlook or beliefs. This strong family bond, extended beyond the immediate family to all Jews, was the secret of Jewish survival and success throughout the ages. Unfortunately, the opposite is also true: The erosion of the Jewish family and its age-old traditions and values has caused vast assimilation and division in our ranks. Yet we are beginning to see the tide reversing somewhat, and once again there is increased emphasis on family values and a renewed interest in tradition. This effort to strengthen the family based on Jewish values is vital in our age.

This section of the book deals with relationships that are the building blocks of a Jewish home.

11 Marriage

One of the basic foundations of Jewish civilization is the institution of marriage. Family structure is built upon a couple — a man and woman — who join in life and build a Jewish home. The paradigm for this relationship of marriage is the Biblical description of Adam and Eve in the Garden of Eden. The Lord, so to speak, performed this original marriage ceremony and thereby set the pattern for Jewish and all human personal life. The Torah states flatly that, "it is not good for people to be alone." Marriage is therefore not just reproduction and physical fulfillment, it is caring and companionship. (An old Hungarian saying, which seems to properly balance cynicism and realism, states: "The best thing about marriage is that you are never alone, and the worst thing about marriage is that you are never alone.") Bearing out the brief Torah statement on marriage are the numerous statistics showing that married people, on the average, live longer and are healthier than people who live alone.

In Jewish life, marriage is seen as a holy institution. Though divorce is permissible in Judaism when there are irreconcilable differences between husband and wife, the institution of marriage is viewed as being one of permanence, requiring constant effort, personal adaptation and growth. Marriage, in Jewish thought, is always a work in progress. Viewed that way, marriage is neither dull nor static, but rather a relationship that is constantly renewing itself — full of discovery and even adventure.

Methods of finding a spouse vary in different Jewish societies. The *shidduch* system of arranged introductions is popular among many religious populations. There are various levels of "arrangement." Among some groups, the fully arranged marriage is extant; i.e. the parents of the bride and groom introduce them to each other with the expectation that the couple will learn to love each other after their nuptials. However, the most common form of *shidduch* is when friends, relatives or parents recommend prospective spouses one to another. On some occasions, amateur or professional *shadchanim* (matchmakers) suggest an appropriate candidate. At that point, the man and woman (and/or their parents) find out more about the prospective spouse through references to determine if the relationship has a realistic chance of success. If so, then the couple meets and the courting procedure begins. The decision whether to marry is left directly to the couple involved. The unwritten rule in this form of dating is that the couple will date only each other until one or the other rejects furthering the relationship or until they decide to marry.

And then there is the method of meeting one's spouse on one's own initiative, whether by chance or at a gathering specifically for singles. In any event, no matter what the method of meeting or arranging, there is no justification in Judaism for forced or coerced marriages. Even in "fully arranged" matches, the consent of the couple involved is mandatory. Since trust in parental judgment still reigns in societies ascribing to this system, and because it is the honorable social norm to be married through firm prior arrangements, the consent of the couple is usually forthcoming.

The wedding ceremony itself (See Chapter 6 for a fuller description.) consists of two introductory blessings over a cup of wine from which the bride and groom both drink. The groom then places a ring on the index finger of the right hand of the bride and declares: "You are hereby sanctified unto me according to the laws of Moses and Israel." Then the *ketubah* (marriage contract) is read publicly, outlining the mutual physical, emotional and financial obligations of the couple to one another. In many instances, it is customary for the rabbi performing the ceremony or for a close relative or friend to extend a few words of congratulations and blessing as well. Then the *Sheva Brachot*, the seven blessings of marriage are recited, again over a cup of wine. These blessings recall the first marriage in the Garden of Eden, the hope for Jewish redemption, wishes for joy and happiness for the bride and groom, and praise for the Creator Who has fashioned man and woman and joins them together in marriage. After these blessings, the couple drinks from the cup of wine.

The ceremony is actually over, but customarily a glass is shattered (beneath the groom's foot) at this point, in memory of the destruction of the Temple in Jerusalem. This practice is in keeping with the vow taken by the Jews as they went into exile from the Land of Israel, "If I forget you, O Jerusalem, let my right hand forget its skill, let my tongue adhere to my palate — if I fail to *raise Jerusalem above my foremost joy.*"

Great shouts of "Mazal tov" fill the air. Jewish tradition enjoins everyone to participate in rejoicing with the bride and groom in their happiness. A Jewish wedding is not only a personal milestone. It is a national affirmation of the future of the Jewish nation. It is the beginning of a new Jewish home, dedicated to the tenets of Judaism and the fulfillment of no less than the historic mission of the entire Jewish People.

12 Intimacy

Judaism treats sexuality as a natural part of human personality and life. Unlike other religions that view celibacy as a goal of purity and sexual abstinence as a sign of religious piety, Judaism sees a satisfying and natural sexual relationship as the basis of a stable and successful marriage.

Because intimacy is viewed in Judaism as an act that is to be sanctified, sexual relationships outside of marriage are not condoned. Sexual liaisons which are without permanence, shared life goals or true legitimacy are destructive of family life, and reduce the concept of physical intimacy to its most primitive, animalistic form. Just as Jews consciously sanctify the act of eating food through the recitation of blessings, so too, the physical aspect of sexual intimacy requires consciousness of a sacred dimension. Promiscuity, adultery, womanizing, prostitution and all other forms of wanton sexual behavior lack this sacred dimension and are judged to be inherently wrong. They are forbidden in Jewish tradition as the antithesis of a moral life.

The sexual victimization of anyone — man, woman or child — is expressly forbidden in Judaism, including within a marriage. It is considered a heinous and particularly offensive transgression of Torah norms and values. Sexual relations are not only to be consensual and within the framework of marriage, they are to be tinged with holiness. A true personal bonding and the creation of a lasting, mutually satisfying relationship are its primary goals.

In order to infuse a sense of the sacred into the earthiest of human acts, the Torah created a mechanism that guarantees passion and nobility in the fulfillment of physical intimacy. The practice of *taharat hamishpachah* — literally, family purity — has stood as the bedrock of Jewish marriage from Biblical times till today. A twelve-day period occurs approximately *every* month, coinciding with the onset of menstruation and a week thereafter, when the married couple abstains from physical intimacy and marital relations. At the end of this period of days, the wife immerses herself in the purifying waters of a *mikvah* — a pool of water fed from natural sources (such as rainwater, springs or melted snow) — and then returns to the conjugal life of marriage. The period of time that relations are prohibited have nothing to do with physical uncleanness or ancient taboo. It is rooted in spiritual principles, and thus the purifying agent must meet the specific requirements of the *mikvah*, not merely a bathtub or swimming pool.

Spiritually refreshed, she returns to her husband after their twelve-day separation. This mechanism allows for a constant renewal of love and tenderness for one another in the marriage. The act of physical intimacy becomes one of commitment, sensitivity and passion, and not merely lust.

The strength of the Jewish home was always built upon this most holy and private cycle of the relationship between spouses. In my experience as a rabbi, I have found that this concept of *taharat hamishpachah* and its practice has saved many a foundering marriage. It strengthens all spousal relationships.

While it is not a magic bullet to cure all marital strife and discord, it certainly builds a strong base for consideration and cooperation between the spouses. It is a powerful antidote to the sexual dysfunction that marks much of the Western world today.

Physical intimacy is always viewed within the context of family and Jewish continuity. Because our lives are to be lived in a fulfilling, harmonious framework, Judaism does not allow any human activity to be viewed in a vacuum, purely by itself, so to speak. Homosexuality, and other sexual behaviors that are counter to traditional nuclear family-building, and therefore do not promote generational continuity, are opposed by the Torah and Jewish tradition.

Sexual behavior is always a private matter. But it is not so private that it is not subject to Jewish standards, norms and goals. The goal of Judaism to create a "kingdom of priests and a holy nation" remains a paramount interest of Jewish life. The holiness of our nation is dependant upon the holiness of our families, even in our most intimate moments.

13 Children

he Biblical imperative to Adam and Eve to "be fruitful and multiply" remains a core value in Jewish life. Children are seen as a special blessing that guarantees the immortality of the individual family into which they are born and of the human race generally. At the same time, they create enormous responsibilities for parents. Only human offspring have such a long childhood and are dependent on their parents for survival and growth for many years.

In Jewish life, this responsibility of parents to their children is emphasized and given very high priority. The health, sustenance, education and overall well-being of a child are inescapable responsibilities of Jewish parenthood. Instilling Torah values and knowledge in children is of major importance as "... You shall teach your children," is one of God's commandments to the Jewish People. Even high-priced tuition payments to Jewish schools do not automatically discharge this responsibility.

The home environment, the behavior of parents toward their children and toward each other, unconditional love, respect and nurturing are all crucial factors in raising a Jewish child.

As a precious and fragile vessel, a child must be handled delicately, carefully and with wisdom and foresight. Parents should strive to instill a sense of self-worth, pride of identity and uniqueness in their children. The caricature of the martyred Jewish mother, nagging, threatening and instilling deep guilt feelings in her children is both unfair and damaging. Nevertheless, this erroneous stereotype does have an instructive purpose: It should warn us that those qualities and character traits in parents should be avoided at all costs.

Emotional, verbal and physical abuse is not in accordance with the Torah and Jewish values. Tragically, it has been shown that parents who abuse children produce children who are also likely to abuse their own children. There may be times that a good love tap on the child's posterior can do a world of good for everyone concerned, but such circumstances are the rare exception and certainly are not recommended as an established family policy to be implemented at will. All children do certainly provoke parents at times. Anger and abuse are not the correct responses to that frustration. As the saying goes, "Honey catches more flies than vinegar," and this is true especially where children are concerned.

Yet the Torah always teaches balance. Parents should not give in to the temptation of satisfying every whim and desire of the child. The Bible informs us that King David brought upon himself the rebellion and attempted coup by his son because "his father (David) never withheld anything from him during his youth." There is a great deal of latitude between being an oppressive and domineering parent and spoiling a child. Every parent has to determine where that line should be drawn for each individual child.

Each child in a family is a world unto himself or herself. No two human beings, even children born to the same mother and father and raised in the same home environment, are ever the same.

The Talmud teaches us that, "Just as no two people are completely identical physically, so too do they differ regarding their opinions and outlook on life." The wise parent will certainly realize this. Not all children in one family should attend the same school, pursue the same career, be held to one rigid, inflexible standard of scholarship, achievement or deportment. This is especially true in large families where the challenges of parenthood are often even more daunting.

The number of children in a family is not a barometer of the success of the marriage or of the happiness of the parents. On the other hand, there are no statistics indicating that a large family is less likely to produce well-adjusted people than a small family. When there are more children, there are certainly more challenges and responsibilities. In a house of love and warmth, consideration and sensitivity, there will certainly be enough goodness to go around for all.

14 Divorce

While Judaism views marriage and family as the basic unit in the structure of civilization, it never demands that two people stay married to each other in every circumstance. The Torah provides a divorce mechanism as a practical solution to an otherwise intractable relationship problem. Thus, throughout Jewish history, divorce was present as an option for ending an unsatisfactory family relationship. However, it was always viewed as a last resort, to be used only after all good faith efforts at adjusting the problems and reconciling the people involved had been exhausted. Though there is no statistical proof, it is nonetheless clear that divorce was relatively uncommon in Jewish society until the latter part of the twentieth century. There are many reasons why this is true.

A primary reason is that divorce itself was considered somewhat scandalous in general society, and Jews tend to abide by the mores of society in their locality. In the latter half of the twentieth century, when divorce became acceptable and common in general society, it also became much more accepted and prevalent among Jews.

The wisdom of Judaism is that not all marriages can be saved and couples are not doomed to live out their lives together in mutual misery. However, divorce on demand, so to speak, is also not a wise course, especially when there are children involved. Thus, every case has to be judged individually and in accord with its particular circumstances.

The Talmud discusses what behaviors or attitudes constitute grounds for divorce. Opinions vary, with a wide range of views expressed, from very serious grounds (infidelity) to simple tiredness of the relationship. In a Jewish bill of divorce — in Hebrew, known as a *get* — no grounds for the granting of the divorce are mentioned. The *get*, always twelve lines long, is handwritten by a scribe specifically for the couple involved in the divorce, though the text is standard for all cases, with the only mandatory differentiations being the date of the divorce, the exact names of the parties (including Hebrew and non-Hebrew names, nicknames and/or contractions of the original names), and the place where the bill of divorce was written and duly witnessed (a city, town or locality near an identifiable, permanent body of water). Two specific witnesses must sign and attest to the validity of the bill of divorce and to the agreement of the parties that the bill of divorce is being given and accepted of their own free will and volition.

It takes about an hour to handwrite the bill of divorce. In my rabbinic experience, I have seen couples try and reconcile within that time period, thus obviating the need to deliver the bill of divorce. That is undoubtedly what the rabbis had in mind in drawing out the ceremony and the writing of the divorce document. After the scribe and the witnesses have finished their tasks, the divorce document is given to the wife by the husband. The document is then returned to the rabbinical court, which voids it so that it cannot be used for a different instance of couples with the same names. The rabbinical court then issues a certificate of divorce — a *ptur* — to each of the parties. Should either of them wish to marry in the future, this document must be presented to the officiating rabbi.

Rabbinical divorce courts also adjudicate property rights, custody of children, support payments and other untidy matters that are usually part of a divorce proceeding. Since emotions understandably run high in divorce proceedings and all egos and personalities involved are hurt and bruised, all rabbinical adjudications are subject to criticism from disappointed parties. In rabbinical history, there are famous cases of attempts to overturn divorce results by appealing to another rabbinical court. One such case, concerning a divorce granted in Alsace (Kliva), became a cause célèbre in the eighteenth century Jewish world, eventually involving many of the major rabbinical personalities of Europe.

Today, it often happens that civil courts and rabbinic courts are involved in the same case, causing an increase in friction, misunderstandings and legal fees. Marriage may be an imperfect institution, but divorce is also far from perfect. As in much of life, human beings can only try to do their best in what are often very trying and difficult circumstances.

Year-Round Mitzvot

*J*udaism is a religion of symbols, rituals and commandments. Belief and attitudes will not stand the test of generations and the passage of centuries unless they are reinforced by concrete behavior. Thus the key words in Jewish blessings prior to performing specific mitzvot are: "...That You, God, have commanded us to..." The Talmud teaches us that Judaism is comprised of 613 commandments. Of these, 248 are "positive" commandments that require action on our part — charity, prayer, Torah study, eating matzoh on Passover, etc. The remaining 365 commandments are "negative" commandments that require us to abstain from committing certain behavior — marital infidelity, eating non-kosher food, doing "work" on the Sabbath, etc. Since many of these commandments are related to the Temple service in Jerusalem and the laws of purity associated with that Temple, a good number of them are not applicable today, though with the rebuilding of the Temple in Messianic times they will again come into practical use.

Because of the brief nature of this book, this chapter cannot deal with all of the commandments. Numerous scholarly works exist in English that do deal with the entire gamut of the 613 commandments and the reader is referred to them for further in-depth study of the topic. I have chosen to discuss here only a few basic rituals and commandments that are representative of the whole. These commandments are basic to Jewish life style and homes. In fact, they are living representations of the traditions of Israel granted to us through Moses at Mount Sinai, practiced throughout the generations in our everyday life.

15 **Ethics**

Judaism is not only a faith system. It is primarily a way of life based upon ethical principles as outlined in the Torah. These ethical values govern a Jew's behavior in all facets of life: family and home; profession and career; interpersonal relationships; government; the marketplace; even driving an automobile. The ethical value system of Judaism is all-inclusive and binding on all Jews and in all aspects of human life. While most Jews do adhere to these principles, the fact that some Jews do not always rise to meet the demands of this system in no way compromises the correctness of the ethical standards of the Torah. One must be astute enough and sufficiently sophisticated not to confuse the behavior and failings of individual Jews with Judaism itself. As in any other area of Judaism, keeping its laws in every detail is a lifelong challenge and pursuit.

Many of the ethical standards of Judaism regarding commerce have become law and the norm in most societies in the world today. The Torah long ago prohibited unfair competition, specious advertising, restraint of trade, monopolies, false weights and measures, unfair labor practices, mistreatment and exploitation of workers, arbitrary withholding of wages or bill payments, and copyright infringement, to mention some of the ethical values that govern the Jewish marketplace.

All business ethics fall under the rubric of the Torah that one is not allowed to take from another what is not rightfully his or hers. That is stealing. Stealing can apply to another person's money, time, talent — even someone else's trust and confidence. No matter what, it is still stealing. The rabbis of the Talmud recognized the failings of humans when it comes to money and therefore ruefully declared, "Most people are guilty of some sort of theft in their lifetime." Being put on notice as to the standard of ethics that the Torah sets for us in our commercial dealings can help mitigate that bitter judgment of human behavior.

In the field of medicine and healing, Judaism also established a code of ethical behavior. The supremacy of life itself is the cornerstone of all ethical behavior. In today's world of advanced medical technology — of organ transplants and breathing respirators, etc. — the questions that arise on medical ethics have become ever more important and ever more complicated. Major works of Torah scholarship have been published over the past few decades to deal with these questions of life and death.

In Jewish tradition, a physician is seen as doing God's work, so to speak. It is no coincidence that the Jewish doctor has been a fixture of all societies in the world for many centuries. Because of this Jewish Torah connection to medicine, Jewish law insists that the medical practitioner must be protected from unwarranted legal and social harassment while at the same time being held to the highest professional and ethical standards of proficiency and quality care. How to balance these two delicate and sometimes contradictory values remains the challenge of Jewish law and Jewish life. But again, the difficulty of realizing the practicality of balancing such ethical norms in no way compromises the standards of ethical behavior that the Torah has described for us in these matters.

Ethical behavior between people is a given in Jewish life. There are strong prohibitions against slanderous speech; against defamation of character; against insults and abuse, whether verbal or physical; and against demeaning others because of their lack of education, talent or wealth. The Jewish concept of charity and philanthropy is based on the ethical imperative of caring for others. Charity is not limited to contributing money. It includes tending and visiting the sick, comforting the bereaved, extending hospitality towards visitors, being kind to the very young and the aged and feeling a sense of responsibility towards the needs of others.

Respect and tolerance of other human beings, even of those who believe differently than one's self, are all part of the Jewish ethical makeup. Standing up for justice and right, for freedom and equality of opportunity, for concern for life and universal knowledge are also the components of Jewish ethical behavior. The task of every Jew, as of every human being in this world, is to be an ethical person. The Torah and Jewish tradition define such a person and facilitate an ethical system of life based on proper values.

16 Kosher Food

ne of the distinguishing features of Jewish law and life is the concept of dietary laws. Jews are bidden to eat food that is "kosher." The Torah lists general rules that govern which foods are kosher. As far as meat is concerned, the meat of animals that chew their cud and have split hooves is permissible. Thus meat from animals such as rabbit, swine and horses is forbidden fare, while venison is permitted.

Swine meat — pork, ham, etc. — especially has been a symbol of "anti-Jewish" food. This is because those who persecuted Jews throughout the ages, from the Greeks to Hitler, coerced Jews to eat swine meat. Stalin's minions forced Jews into collective farms that raised swine exclusively. Thus an emotional aversion to swine meat beyond just the original ritual religious prohibition arose in Jewish life.

Poultry such as chicken, goose, duck and turkey is permitted under Jewish law. Even more exotic birds, such as quail and partridge, are also permissible, but are not usually found in kosher homes.

In order for the meat or poultry to be kosher, the animal or bird has to be slaughtered in a ritual fashion. This procedure requires the severing of the trachea and esophagus by a sharp, smooth blade. The blade is not allowed to have any nicks in it and must be wielded in a continuously smooth backwards and forwards thrusting motion. The person wielding the blade is a *shochet*, a ritual slaughterer, specially trained for the task of preparing properly smooth and sharp blades and performing the slaughter quickly, expertly and with minimum pain to the animal or bird. After slaughter, the inner organs of the animal or bird are inspected. If these are found to be diseased (including tumors, infections, punctures, etc.), the animal is *treif*, i.e. not kosher. The word *treif*, which originally only referred to this type of faulty internal organ problem, has since been expanded to mean any food that is not kosher.

Due to the Torah's prohibition against eating or drinking blood, the meat and poultry that we eat is partially deveined of blood arteries and veins. Capillary blood is removed by a process of soaking the meat or poultry in water; then the meat is salted to draw forth any remaining blood. After approximately an hour, the blood-soaked salt is washed away and the meat is then ready to be cooked. An alternative method of removing the blood from the meat is by broiling it over an open fire or heating element. Those who are not allowed to consume salt may use this alternative method of removing the blood.

Seafood is also subject to the laws of kosher dining and food. Fish that have fins and scales are kosher. Fish without scales, and other seafood such as shellfish, shrimp, crab, lobster and turtle, are all not kosher.

Milk is permissible only from kosher animals that have split hooves and chew their cud, such as cows and goats. Milk and meat foods are not to be mingled in cooking or eating.

Baked goods may or may not be kosher, depending upon the shortening and other ingredients that they contain. Wine and grape products also must be manufactured under kosher supervision. All types of wine — red, white, sweet, dry — can be kosher if manufactured under kosher supervision.

Many reasons for the observance of kosher food have been advanced over the ages. The "reasons" vary from those of healthy diet to opposition to prevailing pagan customs. All of these reasons have some element of accuracy within them, but none of them really explain the Torah's demand that Jews eat only kosher food. Traditionally, Jews believe that the kosher rule is one of the few laws that are given to us without a reason understandable by man. It is observed because God commanded it, not for any physical or social benefits that happen to be in vogue.

Suffice it to say that the observance of the kosher laws has been a hallmark of the Jewish people throughout the ages. In homes and communities where the discipline of *kashrut* has remained strong, so has the continuity and growth of the Jewish community. The spiritual reasons for *kashrut* may remain hidden from us, but the practical holding power of *kashrut* observance for individual Jews and the Jewish people collectively are obvious.

MEAT AND MILK

Included in the discipline of the dietary laws of the Torah is the prohibition of cooking and/or eating foods of dairy and meat origins at the same time. The original verse in the Torah concerning the subject is cryptic and discusses one particular instance of the law: "Do not cook a kid in its mother's milk." By Jewish tradition from Sinai, and as later developed by rabbinic expansion and explanation of the matter, all of the laws preventing the mixing of meat and milk in Jewish life were derived from that taut sentence in the Torah.

Maimonides explains that the Torah intentionally described this broad issue in the narrow terms of "not to cook a kid in its mother's milk," since this practice of cooking young goats in their mother's milk was a common practice in pagan worship in the ancient world. Thus the basis for the prohibition of mixing milk and meat foods in Jewish law is a further rejection of pagan practice and belief, over and above the basic Torah law forbidding the mixing of meat and milk in itself. The above is an example of giving rational explanations for Divine decrees that in the last analysis defy explanation. Maimonides' explanation certainly was valid for a society threatened by paganism and its practices. However, in a different world, it may appear to be anachronistic. Therefore, the traditional Jewish view is that these laws are Divine decrees (that mortals cannot understand on their truest, deepest levels) that impose a certain discipline upon the Jewish nation. These laws are therefore valid and binding in all times and places. It may well be that the discipline itself that these laws foster is the ultimate earthly reward for their observance.

This Torah rule regarding milk and meat became the hallmark of the Jewish kitchen throughout the ages. Separate dishes, tableware, pots, pans, cleansing and scrubbing pads and even tablecloths, dish towels and table mats for meat and milk foods were always required. Lately, as our kitchens have become larger and better equipped, separate sinks and electric kitchen appliances for milk and meat food preparations have become common in Jewish homes. The tradition in all Jewish homes was to mark the dairy tableware in a manner that would identify it as being different from its meat counterpart. Most Jewish homes today have different patterns of tableware to differentiate between the two and use different colors to distinguish between the fabrics and cleansing pads used for milk or meat.

Dairy and meat foods may not be eaten together at the same meal. There are various customs concerning the eating of meat after just eating dairy foods. There is a custom that allows meat to be eaten immediately after milk foods, but requires the person eating that food to first rinse his or her mouth from any residue of the milk food. Another custom requires that (in addition to rinsing the mouth) a half hour wait intervene between completing the eating of the dairy foods and the later eating of meat. There is also a custom that requires the recitation of Grace After Meals between the eating of milk and meat thereafter.

However, *all* customs agree that milk cannot be eaten immediately after meat foods. The prevailing custom is to wait six hours after eating meat before eating dairy foods. A variant of this custom, one that was common among the Jews of Provence in the Middle Ages and Lithuania in the nineteenth century, is to wait into the sixth hour, meaning five hours plus some minutes. There is also a custom, prevalent amongst descendants of German Jews, to wait only three hours after eating meat before eating dairy foods. Another custom, restricted to the Jews of Holland, was to wait only one hour between the meat meal and the eating of dairy foods. The Talmud records that there were pious Jews who did not eat both milk and meat foods within the same twenty-four hour period of time. In all instances, the Jewish people were careful never to eat milk foods immediately after eating meat dishes, let alone at the same time.

In our times, questions regarding the use of the same dishwashers, stovetops, ovens, etc. for both meat and dairy foods have arisen. There is much rabbinic responsa (rabbis' answers to Jewish legal questions posed to them) and opinion regarding all of these questions. For millennia, classical rabbinic responsa has always dealt with the accidental mixing of meat and dairy dishes and tableware, of drops of milk falling somehow into quarts of meat or chicken soup, and of other such questions regarding the separation of milk and meat utensils. In preparing for rabbinic ordination, the section of study regarding these issues is one of the most intensive and complex subjects taught.

Because of the expertise required to competently answer questions of this nature, Jewish men and women have always sought rabbinic guidance when these questions arise. They know that in doing so, they are safeguarding one of the hallmarks of the Jewish home. Though the observance of these *kashrut* laws has been eclipsed in some Jewish societies for a number of years, there is currently a return to this basic mode of Jewish identification and observance.

KASHRUT CERTIFICATION

An enormous number of the products on the shelves of all supermarkets in the Western world are kosher and are certified to be so by various kosher certifying agencies. Their certification attests to the fact that no animal fat derivative or other non-kosher ingredient was used in the production of the food item and that the product was manufactured under rabbinic supervision. Almost all of the *kashrut* certification agencies have a distinctive symbol appearing on the label of the product, attesting to the food product meeting its kosher standards.

The largest *kashrut* certification agencies in the world are the various rabbinates in Israel that certify kosher products to the Israeli market as well as for export. Almost all manufactured food products in Israel are certified kosher. The largest *kashrut* certification agency outside of Israel is that of the Union of Orthodox Jewish Congregations of America. Its *kashrut* symbol — the Ⓤ — appears on thousands of food products. It also provides *kashrut* supervision for the industrial raw materials such as food-grade glycerin that are used in the manufacture of thousands of food products in America and around the world. The OU is a non-profit organization headquartered in New York City that employs hundreds of *kashrut* field supervisors. Because of its ubiquitous presence in the food market, the OU has enabled Jews to walk into almost any American supermarket and find a wide variety of kosher foods, including meat and poultry products.

Because of the great volume of manufactured products (millions of jars of peanut butter, for example) the expense of kosher supervision to the manufacturer, as amortized on a per unit basis, is small. *Kashrut* supervision costs are usually assigned to the advertising budget of the product (as the kosher symbol increases sales to Jews and non-Jews) and not to the direct manufacturing cost budget.

There are many privately operated *kashrut* agencies that certify food products as well. These agencies also have their special symbols that appear on the label of the food product. Symbols such as Ⓚ, ⚠, 𝕂 represent these certifying agencies, and there are many more. There are also a number of national rabbinic groups, especially in the Chassidic world, that provide special *kashrut* certification for certain food products, as well as local rabbinic groups and community congregations that are involved in local kosher certification.

Perhaps never before in Jewish history has there been such a variety and quantity of kosher food products and eating establishments available to the kosher consumer. The presence of organized, technically knowledgeable, efficient *kashrut* certifying agencies has truly made *kashrut* observance trouble-free, something that was undreamt of but a century ago.

17 Tallit and Tzitzit

The commandment to wear *tzitzit* — knotted strings on the fringes of a four-cornered garment — is specifically explained in the Torah, "So that [by the wearing of *tzitzit*] you will remember all of My commandments and perform them, and thus be dedicated to the service of the Lord your God." Since the Biblical commandment applies only to four-cornered garments (such four-cornered robes and togas were common dress in ancient and classical times) and since most people no longer wear four-cornered garments, it became obvious that this important commandment was in danger of falling into disuse and eventual oblivion.

Centuries ago, the rabbis introduced the requirement that Jewish males wear a four-cornered garment as part of their daily attire, thereby necessitating their wearing of the knotted strings — *tzitzit* — as well. This four-cornered garment is called *tallit*. (In Hebrew *tallit* simply means a garment.) The *tallit* comes in two forms: the *tallit gadol*, a large *tallit*; and the *tallit katan*, a smaller *tallit*. Both have the same type of *tzitzit* attached to its four corners.

According to Biblical precept, the *tzitzit*, which is composed of four strings folded over to become eight, was to have three white strings and one blue string. The dye for this blue string (called *techelet* in Hebrew) was obtained from the blood pouch of a type of sea snail called *chilazon*. (The blue and white colors and stripes of the flag of the State of Israel were taken from the traditional stripes of the *tallit* and the colors of the *tzitzit*.) After the destruction of the Holy Temple in 70 CE and the subsequent dispersal of the Jews over the globe, the exact type of snail's blood used for the dye was forgotten. Rather than use a dye not commanded in the Torah, only white was used for all four strings of the *tzitzit* for 1,500 years. Over the last century, however, attempts to identify the *chilazon* were made by rabbinic scholars. The prevalent opinion today is that the *chilazon* is the murex trunculus snail. Its blood is processed today in Israel to create the blue dye for *techelet*. There are differences of Jewish legal opinion as to whether the availability of this dye constitutes reason to change the custom of 1,500 years of having all white strings. Therefore, though tens of thousands of Jews today do have the rediscovered Biblical blue string in their *tzitzit*, most Jews continue to wear all-white stringed *tzitzit*.

The *tallit katan* — the smaller *tallit* — is worn every day by Jews during their waking hours. Most Jews wear the *tallit katan* under their shirt as a type of undergarment. Though wearing the *tallit katan* as an undergarment, there are those who wear the *tzitzit* strings outside of their pants. Among certain Chassidic groups, the *tallit katan* is worn over the shirt, though under the jacket or coat. Either way, the reason it is customary for the *tzitzit* to be visible is because the commandment in the Torah mandating the wearing of *tzitizit* stipulates, "...that you may see it and remember all the commandments of God and perform them; and not explore after your heart and [stray] after your eyes..." The purpose of the *tallit katan*, then, is to serve as a constant reminder of God's word and of proper, moral Jewish behavior.

The Talmud is replete with stories of how the wearing of *tzitzit* saved Jews from devastatingly sinful behavior. Avoiding temptation and compromising situations, being aware of our weak tendencies, making a conscious effort to improve ourselves morally and spiritually, are all lessons of *tzitzit*.

The *tallit gadol* — the large *tallit* — is worn during the daily morning service prayers. This garment is reminiscent of a Roman toga, though it is worn draped over the head and the shoulders of the person and not held together in his hand in Roman style. The *tallit gadol* has stripes running its length. In European Jewish societies, these stripes were blue or black in color. Among the Jews of the Mediterranean basin and the Middle East, the stripes were another shade of white. In Germany, even children wore a *tallit gadol* during the morning service. Among other Jewish societies, the *tallit gadol* was donned only after Bar Mitzvah. The prevailing custom in Eastern Europe was for Jews to wear a *tallit gadol* only after marriage. Thus, a *tallit gadol* was and is a customary wedding gift from the bride and/or her family to the groom on their wedding day. In some societies, a decorated collar of silver or embroidery, called an *atarah*, is affixed to the top of the *tallit* to add aesthetic beauty to the holy garment.

All Hebrew letters have numerical equivalents. The numerical value of the Hebrew letters of *tzitzit* is 600. There are five knots and eight strings in the *tzitzit*, thus giving it an overall numerical value of 613, equal to the number of commandments that comprise the Torah. It is no wonder therefore that *tzitzit* are a treasured vehicle of remembering all of God's words and commandments.

18 Tefillin

The Biblical command to "bind them upon your arm as a sign and as frontlets between your eyes" refers to the Jewish practice of wearing *tefillin* (on all days except Sabbath and holidays). *Tefillin* consists of two perfectly square black leather boxes that contain parchments upon which are written four Biblical passages regarding the faith of Israel. They are treated with special respect and accorded unique holiness in Jewish practice. One's mind should be concentrated and aware of their presence on his arm and head. In addition, the body should be cleansed and one's appearance in order when wearing *tefillin*. One is forbidden to relieve himself while wearing *tefillin*. Because of the stringent standards described above for behavior and concentration, the present custom is for men to wear *tefillin* only during the period of the morning prayers. However, in Talmudic times and earlier, they wore *tefillin* the entire day, removing them only when necessary, and then putting them on again later. Even in more modern times, there were special Jews who wore their *tefillin* during as much of the entire day as circumstances would allow. The Talmud placed special emphasis on the observance of wearing *tefillin* and under the most dire of circumstances and greatest of dangers, Jews always struggled to observe this commandment.

One of the boxes is attached to the left arm (the right arm, if the person is left-handed) — opposite the heart — by means of a black leather strap wound around the arm. The other box is held in place on the head — at the mind — by a pair of black straps that run down the front of the person's body to below the waist. The position of the box on the head is centered over the eyes, but the front of the box should only descend to where the hairline is (or once was!). The head box is divided into four separate compartments into which each of four Biblical passages is inserted separately. The two sides of the head box have the Hebrew letter *shin* emblazoned in relief on the leather box itself. On one side, the *shin* has three "legs" and on the other side the *shin* has four "legs." The head box also has a hair from the leather hide that protrudes slightly at the front of the box. The box on the arm has smooth sides and all four passages from the Torah contained within it are written on one piece of parchment that is rolled into a tube to fit the box. All of these specifics are in accordance with accepted Jewish Oral Law from Sinai, since the Written Torah contains no description or explanation of the commandment to "bind them upon your arms...and as frontlets between your eyes." It is the Oral tradition from Sinai that explains all Biblical commandments to us.

Tefillin were always treated as an heirloom in Jewish life. A deceased grandfather's *tefillin* would be refurbished and then worn by a grandson. "My grandfather's *tefillin*" is mentioned in the Talmud as a description of Jewish continuity and sustained spiritual and physical survival. Jewish boys begin their experience with *tefillin* just before their Bar Mitzvah. In fact, putting on *tefillin* is the symbol of coming of age in the Jewish world. The *tefillin* are kept in a special bag, usually embroidered with the name of the owner, and often decorated with a design or picture.

Prices for *tefillin* vary according to size and quality of the parchment, the leather and the workmanship of the scribes who produce them. But *tefillin* are an eternal investment, and their cost is easily amortized over a long span of time. *Tefillin* are the sign, the symbol, of a Jew's attachment to the God and Torah of Israel. They speak to us of our past, of Exodus and of Sinai. They also speak to our future, to our children and grandchildren and their descendants who will continue to "bind them to their arms as a sign and wear them as frontlets to their eyes."

19 Mezuzah

O ne of the most obvious physical symbols of a Jewish home is the presence of a *mezuzah* on its doorposts. The Torah commands Jews to "write these [statements of faith] on the doorposts of your homes and gates." The word *mezuzah* itself literally means the sides of a doorframe. However because of the commandment to "write [these commandments]…" the word *mezuzah* has come to mean the "writings" placed on the doorpost and not only the doorpost itself. The *mezuzah*, as it is commonly called today, is therefore a piece of parchment upon which a scribe has written by hand the main declarations of Jewish faith as quoted in the Torah: the *Shema* ("Hear O Israel, the Lord is our God, the Lord is One."); *V'ahavtah* ("And you shall love the Lord your God…"); and *V'hayah im shamoa* ("If you will listen to My commandments and do My will…").

The size of the parchment can vary, though most scribes prefer a decent sized piece of parchment so that they do not have to engage in micrography when writing the holy words. The parchment is then usually wrapped from right to left in the form of a tube, though this is not strictly required, as the parchment may be used even in its original flat form. On the back of the parchment, three obscure Hebrew words are written that symbolize names of God. These names are not written explicitly but rather with substitute lettering. However, the name of God, *Shadai* (spelled in Hebrew *shin, daled, yud*), is written on the back of the parchment clearly and prominently. When the *mezuzah* is rolled as a tube, it is this name of God that is visible.

Mezuzot are affixed to the entry doors of the house, as well as to the doorways between rooms. The *mezuzah* parchment can be attached to the doorpost in a variety of fashions. In many of the stone homes in Jerusalem, a niche for the *mezuzah* is actually carved out of the stone and the parchment, wrapped as a tube and with a protective clear plastic covering it, is inserted into that niche. However, in most of the Jewish world, the parchment is inserted into a *mezuzah* case and that case is then nailed, screwed or glued to the right hand doorpost of the house. To satisfy a difference of opinion in Jewish law as to whether the *mezuzah* should be mounted to the doorpost in a vertical or horizontal fashion, a happy solution of placing the *mezuzah* case and its contents on the doorpost at a forty-five degree angle (with the top of the *mezuzah* angled inward toward the room) was agreed upon.

The *mezuzah* case has become a source of Jewish inspirational creativity for artisans, designers and craftsmen over the centuries. Every form of material has been employed in the manufacture of *mezuzah* cases, from gold and silver to wood and plastic. In the houses of the wealthy and of art collectors, *mezuzah* cases are often commissioned from leading craftsmen and are unique to that home and family. Most Jews, however, manage with simple materials and plain linear tube design.

Because of the significant words written in it, the *mezuzah* serves as a constant reminder of God's presence in our lives and homes. The custom of Jews is to kiss the *mezuzah* when entering or leaving the home. The *mezuzah* is also regarded as a protective device for the home and for all who live there, but because it is a direct commandment of the Torah, it never was relegated to the status of an amulet.

The *mezuzah* has become one of the most beloved commandments, observed today by a broad segment of the Jewish People. In the State of Israel, almost every Jewish home, office and store has a *mezuzah* on the doorpost. It represents the continuity of Jewish family and generations. It identifies and inspires the Jewish home. It speaks to us about ourselves and our faith when "we go forth and when we come in." As such, it is one of the most powerful symbols of Jewish living.

Prayer

One of the staples of Jewish life is prayer — daily, three times a day, every day. The obligation of prayer is manifest in all Jewish teachings and tradition. The Bible records the prayer traditions of the founders of our People, the Patriarchs and Matriarchs of Israel.

Prayer has many aspects to it, but its main purpose is to provide a conduit of conversation and connection, if you will, between humans and our Creator. Prayer is therefore seen in Judaism as a universal requirement, one not limited to Jews alone. The prophet Isaiah proclaimed, "For My house shall be a house of prayer for all peoples."

Learning how to pray and what to say is a lifelong education. As in almost all other matters of life, Judaism has rules, rituals, advice and guidelines on how to meet this challenge. After all, it is difficult to imagine how one can converse with God. Finite man and the Infinite Lord at first glance don't seem to communicate easily. It is the art of prayer, sometimes mundane, often exalting, but always necessary, that defines our relationship with Him.

This chapter deals with the Jewish form of prayer: when to pray, how to pray and to a certain extent, why to pray. It also deals with the concepts of public *prayer and private prayer, and with the development of synagogue prayer over the centuries. Prayer, in Judaism, is a complex matter, for although it is often public in its form, it is nevertheless eternally private in its true nature. It is through prayer that Jews have found comfort, solace, hope and faith throughout our history. It is a mighty weapon in life – one that should not be allowed to rust away in disuse.*

The Morning Prayer: Shacharit

T he name *Shacharit* is derived from the Hebrew word *shachar,* meaning dawn or morning. According to Jewish tradition, the institution of daily morning prayers was a contribution of our father Abraham, the founder of our faith and people. It is written in the Bible that Abraham awoke early in the morning to address his God. The concept of saying a morning prayer is deeply ingrained in Jewish life. The morning prayers consist firstly of thanks and appreciation for being alive (no small matter!) and for the honor and responsibility of serving God and mankind by being Jewish. It is during the *Shacharit* prayers of the morning that men wear a *tallit* (a large, four cornered cloak with *tzitzit* fringes attached at each of the four corners of the garment) and *tefillin,* the black-boxed phylacteries that are worn daily on the arm and head, except for Shabbat and holidays.

Shacharit consists of a number of sections. After the thanks mentioned above, there appear a number of

Psalms praising the Lord and recounting His wonders and greatness. This section is titled *Pesukei D'zimra* — verses of joyful praise. This order of prayer is in line with the Talmudic concept that before one asks for favors and blessings, one should realize Who is being asked. In this section, historical events such as the Exodus from Egypt and the splitting of the Reed Sea are recalled, and the triumphant Song of Moses upon the deliverance of Israel from the hands of Pharaoh is recited.

The next section of the *Shacharit* prayer service is centered upon the recitation of *Shema Yisrael* — the core prayer of Judaism — "Hear O Israel, the Lord is our God, the Lord is One." There are two blessings that precede the *Shema* prayer, one regarding the wonders of the light of day and the other describing our gratitude for receiving God's Torah at Sinai. After *Shema*, there is a blessing thanking God for our past redemptions and survival, as well as entreaties to the Almighty for the future redemption of Israel and all mankind.

The next part of the service consists of the nineteen-blessing *Amidah*, which is recited in a hushed voice, standing at attention. Encapsulated within that prayer are all of our possible requests to the Lord for health, prosperity, peace and a just world. Additional personal requests and entreaties may be added to the standard ritual text to fit one's situation. The *Amidah* is repeated out loud for the benefit of the congregation. The service then continues with the penitential prayer *Tachanun*, consisting of Psalms and verses asking for forgiveness of sin. On Mondays and Thursdays a lengthier version of *Tachanun* is said, as well as the reading of the first part of the Torah portion of the week from the Torah scroll. The service concludes with a number of additional Psalms and verses that ask for Divine help in the day's forthcoming tasks. This is followed by the Psalm of the Day that was recited and sung by the Levites in the Temple in Jerusalem. In fact, the entire *Shacharit* service is a replacement for the morning sacrifice service that opened the daily Temple service in Jerusalem.

Prayer is an excellent way to begin the day. It focuses a person's thoughts on the true priorities in life and gives one the spiritual strength to face the mundane and often vexing problems of everyday existence. At one time, Jews were awakened to pray by a designated person who knocked at the door, calling: "Rise up to serve the Lord, our Creator." Such doorknockers may be relics of our past, but the morning prayer service remains as the foundation stone of a Jew's entire day.

The Afternoon Prayer: 21 Minchah

Jews are bidden to pray three times daily to the Lord. The *Shacharit* prayer takes place in the morning. It is the longest of the three daily prayers and contains within it the basic affirmations of Judaism — the *Shema*, the *Amidah* and the ideas of repentance, self-improvement and loyalty to God and Israel. The *Maariv* prayer takes place at night, after sunset. It is much shorter in length than *Shacharit*, but nevertheless includes within it the basic *Shema* and *Amidah* prayers. The shortest prayer service of the day takes place in the afternoon, or at least just before sunset, and is called *Minchah*. It is usually a ten to fifteen minute prayer service, but for much of the Jewish world, it has become almost a forgotten prayer. It is not the abbreviated length of *Minchah* that has caused its neglect but rather its inconvenience in coming in the middle of a busy working afternoon. Yet I believe that its importance and necessity lie in that fact alone.

The origins of our three daily prayer services are attributed to our patriarchs, Abraham, Isaac and Jacob. Abraham created the prayer time for *Shacharit*, Isaac for *Minchah* and

Jacob for *Maariv*. The rabbis of the Talmud deduced the role of Isaac in creating *Minchah* from the verse in the Torah that tells us that, "Isaac went out to converse in the field." Converse with whom? The Torah itself is silent on the subject. The rabbis are of the opinion that the conversation was between Isaac and God. And since the Torah describes this event as happening "before evening," Jewish tradition placed the time of *Minchah* as being in the afternoon before sunset. *Minchah* is also connected with being "in the field." *Shacharit* and *Maariv* may be prayed without the time constraints of our mundane everyday tasks. Not so *Minchah*. It stops us in the middle of work, shopping, school and all other usual tasks that life places upon us. It meets us "in the field," at our desks and in our factories.

This timing renders *Minchah* an oasis of spiritual time in a tough workday, a moment of contemplation, a time for a calming of nerves and of focusing priorities. As such, it is perhaps the most important and meaningful prayer service of the day.

Today, there are many *Minchah* prayer groups in companies, stores, colleges, hospitals and in geographic areas of cities where a considerable number of observant Jews are to be found. When I was a lawyer many decades ago in downtown Chicago, there were few, if any, such *Minchah* prayer groups. I would lock myself in my office, tell my secretary that I was making an important private long distance call, and then pray. Many times I felt a sense of rejuvenation and exhilaration after this fifteen minute prayer break. It helped me overcome the disappointments and frustrations that are the daily lot of all of us at our places of work.

What is lacking in much of current Jewish life, even among those who are nominally affiliated with synagogues or Jewish organizations, is a sense of personal participation in Judaism — its rituals, its values and its blessings. We are members, but not participants. No sermon, article, book or class can connect one to feeling truly Jewish in one's inner soul to the extent that a simple *Minchah* prayer can in the midst of a busy afternoon. It creates an opportunity to experience spirit and holy transcendence in daily human life. It can literally change the way we think about people, the world, life, ourselves. It is an experience that no Jew should miss.

The Evening Prayer: 22 Maariv

The night prayer service is called *Maariv*. The word is derived from the Hebrew word *erev*, meaning evening or night. The noun *erev* was converted into a verb — *maariv* — which means literally "bringing on evening/night" and the term is used to denote the prayer itself. The prayer is also called *Arvit*, which is the noun form of the night prayer.

The prayer service consists of two main sections. The first is the recitation of *Shema Yisrael*, the classic Jewish affirmation of faith and loyalty to one God and to Judaism. The recitation of *Shema* at the night prayer services is preceded by two blessings and succeeded by another two blessings, somewhat analogous to the prayer order of the recitation of the *Shema* in the morning *Shacharit* services. The *Shema* is recited twice daily in our prayer services in accordance with the Biblical injunction to say it when "you lie down (night) and when you arise (morning)."

The other part of the evening service is the recitation of the nineteen blessings of *Amidah*, the prayer series that is part of all weekday prayer services. However, there is no repetition by the leader of the service of the *Maariv Amidah*, as there is for *Shacharit* and *Minchah*, the morning and afternoon prayer services respectively.

The service concludes with *Aleinu*, the affirmation of our willingness to serve God and to strive for the betterment of humankind. This prayer ends all of the other (morning and afternoon) prayer services as well. It was originally composed by Joshua after the conquest of Jericho and was restored and revised by Rav Abba, a second century Babylonian Talmudic sage. Due to the majesty of its prose and its exalted content it is also included as part of the *Musaf* (additional) *Amidah* prayer service for Rosh Hashanah and Yom Kippur.

Jewish tradition ascribes the origin of night prayer to our forefather, Jacob. Fleeing the unjustified wrath of his brother Esau, alone and defenseless in attempting to reach the house of his uncle Lavan in Mesopotamia, Jacob rests overnight in an open field with a rock as a pillow under his head. There he prays to the God of his fathers, Abraham and Isaac, for Divine protection and for the opportunity to eventually return safely home to the Land of Israel. This marks the institution of night prayer in Judaism.

There is discussion in the Talmud whether this night prayer is voluntary or mandatory, as are the morning and afternoon prayer services. The basis for this discussion is the fact that the daily morning and afternoon prayers of Israel represent and substitute for the morning and afternoon sacrifices that were offered in Jerusalem in Temple times. However, there were no offerings made in the Temple during the night; thus the *Maariv* service has no Temple antecedent and hence could be deemed a voluntary service. Nevertheless, since the night service originated with our father Jacob, the Jewish people were loath to relegate it to a purely personal and voluntary level. Since Talmudic times onwards, the Jewish people have treated *Maariv* as no less an obligation than *Shacharit* and *Minchah*. However, to remind us that there were no offerings in the Temple at night, the *Amidah* is not repeated publicly by the leader of the services at *Maariv*, as already mentioned above.

The time for praying *Maariv* is directly connected to precisely when night begins, a question in Jewish law. Legal opinions vary from one and a quarter hours (based on a twelve-hour day) before sunset to as much as ninety minutes after sunset. Local latitudinal conditions, exigencies in security and in obtaining a quorum, among other factors, figure in the differing customs of Jewish communities as to the time for *Maariv*. In all circumstances, the *Shema* must be recited again when it is certainly night, in the event that the *Maariv* service took place earlier than actual night.

Because of the darkness and lack of clarity, night became the symbol of exile and persecution in Jewish history. Perhaps because *Maariv* was instituted by Jacob as he fled his homeland to dangers unknown, the prayer is regarded as a symbol of hope and trust in God forevermore. It is no wonder that Jews adopted the obligation of *Maariv* as mandatory. Conversation with the Creator — the prayer service of *Maariv* — helps one survive the long night and wait for the first shaft of light signaling dawn — and the Jewish deliverance for which we still yearn.

23 Cantors

The role of the cantor/*chazan* in today's synagogue world is pretty well defined. His primary task is to lead the congregational services, chanting the prayers and singing the hymns that constitute the Jewish ritual of prayer. However, the role of the cantor has undergone much change in the history of Jewish society. The word *chazan,* which today is fairly exclusively used to mean the cantor of the congregational synagogue, originally signified a much more powerful position. In the Talmud and in Geonic literature, even till the tenth century, the word *chazan* signified the official head of the congregation who had spiritual influence and practical powers. However, by the twelfth century among Ashkenazic Jews, the word *chazan* came to occupy its present meaning as the title of the cantor who leads the prayer services. Among Sephardic communities the word *chazan* continued to describe people with actual power in the congregation almost until our generation.

Naturally, one of the requirements to serve as a cantor is to have a pleasant singing voice. However, in nineteenth century Eastern Europe, a market developed for cantors with outstanding voices and the ability to compose special melodies for the prayer services. Large synagogues in major Jewish centers vied for the services of these outstanding cantors. Many of them were people of piety and faith, as befit their role. Others, however, had little moral or religious standing and were nothing more than entertainers, albeit performing in the holy synagogue instead of the secular concert hall.

It became customary in the early generations of American Jewish life in the late nineteenth and early twentieth centuries for synagogues to employ noted cantors for the High Holy Days and to charge admission for attendance at those services. Among the great cantors of that era were Yossele Rosenblatt, Shaul Kvartin, Pierre Pinchik, Leibele Waldman, Mordechai Hershman and Berele Chagy. To the immigrant Jews, these *chazanim*/cantors were the "stars" of the Jewish world. Noted Jewish vaudeville entertainers such as Eddie Cantor (fitting name) and Al Jolson began their singing careers as cantors before leaving the Jewish world for fame and success in radio and movies. Yossele Rosenblatt himself made a number of movies intended solely for the Jewish market. He also dabbled with the possibility of becoming an opera singer, though that career never really materialized for him. However, for Jan Peerce and Richard Tucker, both of whom remained cantors even after reaching the stage of the New York Metropolitan Opera, famous operatic careers ensued.

Because of this change in the role and perception of the cantor, many devout congregations shied away from "stars" and engaged *baalei tefillah* (literally, masters of prayer) to lead their services. These men were not professional cantors but rather people noted for their melodious voices and fervor of prayer. Whereas cantors could now command respectable fees and salaries, the *baalei tefillah* were usually volunteers or people who received only modest sums for their services. Their role was (and is) viewed not as people who pray while the congregation listens, but as people capable of inspiring *every* member of the congregation to participate in more heartfelt prayers themselves.

The "star" category of cantors is limited today to a relatively few congregations in America, Israel, South Africa and South America. However, the love for cantorial music has undergone a major revival in the past decades. Concerts and cruises featuring cantorial entertainment are very well patronized and many old recordings of great *chazanim* of the past have been digitalized and reissued.

Most congregations that employ a cantor today assign him other duties in the congregation as well. Though the role and definition of the cantor has changed over the centuries, the necessity for the position itself remains as valid in today's Jewish society as before.

24 The Blessing of Dew

uring the months between Passover and Succot, according to the custom of all in Israel and according to the custom of those who follow the Sephardic ritual prayer in the Diaspora, a prayer for dew is inserted in the *Amidah* — the main portion of the daily prayers. Whereas in the winter months there is a prayer for rain, the fact that it rarely, if ever, rains in the Land of Israel from May to September necessitates a change in the prayer from rain to dew in the summer months. In the summer, dew is the lifeline of vegetation in Israel. Every summer morning when I take my daily ten-minute walk to the synagogue, I am impressed by the moisture that is apparent on the grass and bushes that I pass on the way to my synagogue. Where does that moisture come from? There are no automatic sprinkler systems in most of the gardens here. The moisture is a product of the magical dew that appears every dawn throughout God's world.

The necessity for water is obvious to all. After the Exodus, the Torah warned the Jewish nation that they are entering the Land of Israel, a land that depends upon winter rains and underground aquifers and springs. The Torah specifically states that there is no Nile River that will irrigate the land. Therefore, the agricultural bounty of Israel is dependent upon God's blessings from nature — rain and dew. The fact is, however, that this dependence is a blessing in itself! It motivates us to focus on our relationship with the Creator at all times.

Thus prayers for rain and dew have always been integral to the daily prayer services of the Jewish People. In addition to this daily prayer, on Passover a special prayer service for dew is inserted in the *Musaf* service. On Shmini Atzeret, at the conclusion of the Succot season, another special prayer for rain composes a significant part of that *Musaf* prayer service. These special prayer services have a unique melody to them in the Ashkenazic ritual, a melody that closely resembles the haunting solemnity of the melody of the closing *Neilah* service on Yom Kippur. This melody emphasizes the chronic seriousness of the water situation in the Land of Israel and the obvious necessity for Divine aid in providing a bountiful rainfall and abundant dew.

Modern-day Israel has constructed a national water carrier system that brings water from the Sea of Galilee to other parts of the country for irrigation and drinking purposes. Because the rainfall in Israel has been less than usual on average over the past few years and that the demands of the expanding Jewish and non-Jewish population in the country have grown dramatically over the past few years, the level of water in the Sea of Galilee is now quite low and little additional water can be pumped from it without causing serious ecological damage. Other ways must be sought to bring in water when the rainfall and dew are insufficient.

Israel will always have to continue relying on winter rains and summer dew. We have much to pray for in the Jewish world presently, but the prayers for water are always in place.

25 **Kaddish**

One of the best-known prayers in Jewish liturgy is *Kaddish*. This prayer is usually regarded as a memorial prayer for the dead. But that understanding of *Kaddish* is only a half-truth at most. The prayer of *Kaddish* makes no direct reference to death or to memorial type prayers. It is a prayer in the Aramaic language praising God. It also includes the hope for peace and serenity for Israel, as well as the recognition that whatever praise we advance towards God is inadequate to encompass the true greatness of the Creator of us all.

Kaddish forms an integral part of all of the prayer services in Jewish life, irrespective of whether there are mourners present or not. The praise of "the Name of God" is mentioned in the Talmud as being of such priority that doing so with sincere intent alleviates any evil decrees that may befall the person saying it. The word *kaddish* means sanctification and holiness. The prayer itself is thus holy and sanctified to the great Name of God that it extols.

From the fifth century onward, the *Kaddish* prayer also has been used as a vehicle for remembering and "helping" the dead. This usage is based upon a post-Talmudic passage relating that the great Rabbi Akiva once met a stranger on the road. The stranger identified himself to Rabbi Akiva as the spirit of a deceased person who had found no rest for his soul after his death due to his sinful behavior when living in this world. When Rabbi Akiva asked him what the living could do to help him, the stranger told Rabbi Akiva to find his son and ask him to attend the synagogue daily and there publicly praise God's Name. When the son would do this, the deceased's soul would find immortal rest in the spiritual world. Thus the "Mourner's *Kaddish*" became a fixture in Jewish prayer service and life.

The recitation of *Kaddish* in public (i.e. with a *minyan*), and the response of the other worshippers to it in praising God's Name, is considered a deed of such merit that it could aid the soul of the deceased in finding eternal rest and reward, even if the life of the deceased was marred by less than exemplary behavior and attitude. The "Mourner's *Kaddish*" is usually recited at the conclusion of each of the three daily prayer services in the synagogue, and has thus become a strongly emotional family obligation. In the words of the rabbis, "The son brings merit to the soul of the father."

Originally, the "Mourner's *Kaddish*" was recited only by young children mourning the loss of a parent. However, the custom soon included all children of deceased parents, and those mourning other close relatives. The prayer struck such deep roots in Jewish life that an entire corpus of halachic law arose to deal with questions of priority when there are many mourners in the synagogue; how often it should be recited; and other practical issues connected to its public recitation. The "Mourner's *Kaddish*" is recited for eleven or twelve months in memory of parents and for thirty days in memory of all other close relatives.

There is a longer form of the *Kaddish* that is recited after the study of Torah and rabbinic passages. This *Kaddish* is called *Kaddish D'Rabanan* —"the rabbis' *Kaddish*." It is so named because of a paragraph that has been added to the text of the usual *Kaddish*. This paragraph extols the virtues of the rabbinic scholars of Torah and their generations of disciples in the community and throughout Israel. It offers a prayer for their prosperity, health and peace of mind. It is customary for mourners to publicly recite this *Kaddish* as well.

Due to the emotional hold of the concept of the *Kaddish* within Jewish family dynamics, the prayer has taken on an importance and life of its own over the many generations since its inception. *Kaddish* has bound Jewish generations together and facilitated regular synagogue attendance and prayer. Perhaps more than originally contemplated, *Kaddish* has served the purpose of strengthening holiness and indeed honoring Godly service in Jewish life.

The Sabbath

*T*he Sabbath is the keystone of Jewish life. It is no exaggeration to state that throughout Jewish history the term Shomer Shabbat — a Sabbath observer — was the synonym for being Jewish. This definition has undergone strong erosion over the past two centuries: The centrality of the Sabbath in Jewish life weakened when waves of assimilation and utopianism swept over the Jewish world. Destroying the Jews' Sabbath was a target of the Marxist Left when it came to power in Russia as well as in other countries in which Marxism had influence.

But the Sabbath has refused to disappear, and currently it is experiencing an unforeseen revival in Jewish society. The nomination of Senator Joseph I. Lieberman for Vice-President of the United States in the year 2000 is a prime example of how being a Sabbath observer is no longer an impediment: In many ways it has become an asset instead of a liability. But the damage to the Sabbath over the last two centuries has been done. Many Jews today are not intentional "desecrators" of the Sabbath. They are simply oblivious to its existence and unaware of the personal blessings that the holy day can bring to them, to their family and to society generally.

This chapter is intended to provide some insight into the traditional Jewish view of this day of rest and of holiness. However, like most of Judaism, reading or studying about it never equals experiencing the Sabbath day itself in its traditional form.

A Bit of History: Shabbat and the Immigrant Experience

26

The great mass immigration of Jews, mostly from Eastern Europe, to North America from 1870 to 1923 marked a turning point in Jewish history. Never before had there been such a migration of Jews in such numbers and over such a relatively short period of time. In retrospect, one sees the hand of Divine guidance regarding this immigration, for who knows what the fate of world Jewry would have been in the twentieth century if this immigration had not taken place? American Jewry became the largest component of the Jewish People and in many ways it was also the strongest and most influential grouping of Jews in the world. As American Jewry matured, it became increasingly affluent, philanthropic and assimilated. There are clear historical and social reasons for this state of being.

The vast majority of Jews who arrived in North America during this time of mass immigration were Orthodox in practice and in outlook. However, they were in the main not very learned and their Judaism was more of a societal bond than one of true and basic commitment. And there was a strong core of secular and Leftist Jews who had great influence on the lives of these new immigrants. This was certainly true as far as labor unions, *Yiddish* newspapers (such as the *Jewish Daily Forward*) and political organization were concerned. At the time, there was no widespread base of religious Jewish schools; and the afternoon Hebrew School system was doomed to be a failure from its inception. The devotion of the Jewish immigration generation to the American public school system was a major cause of the Americanization of the children of the immigrant generation, their eventual assimilation into American culture and estrangement from Jewish practice and knowledge. Thus, becoming "American" took precedence over remaining "Jewish" for most immigrant families.

The cornerstone of all Jewish life was and still remains the Sabbath. However, Sabbath observance in nineteenth and early twentieth century America was enormously difficult for most of the immigrants. The normal workweek was six days, with Sunday the only day of rest. I remember that as a child growing up on the Jewish West Side of Chicago, I was witness to hundreds of Orthodox Jewish men attending very early Sabbath synagogue services and then getting on the streetcar to go to work. The children of these people, in the main, were no longer Orthodox, did not attend Sabbath synagogue services at all, and were completely non-observant of the Sabbath. Since the Sabbath was the cornerstone of all Jewish family life, it is not surprising that many of the descendants of those immigrants who were forced by economic necessity to work on the Sabbath, no longer identify themselves as members of the Jewish community.

The immigrant generation also insisted that the road to success in American life lay in Jews becoming professionals — physicians, lawyers, accountants, etc. — and not in small trades or as shopkeepers. This attitude still permeates much of American Jewish society, even at a time when the financial rewards of such professionals has dwindled in relation to other fields of endeavor. It was not only the monetary goal that drove the immigrants to send their children into the professions. Rather, it was the status of achievement and acceptance in American life that was the great accomplishment. An immigrant generation is by nature an insecure generation. "My son, the doctor" provided a security blanket that immigrants felt vindicated their changing roles as Jews.

American Jewry is still changing and developing today. It is at one and the same time more Jewish and less Jewish than it has ever been. Only the future will tell us what its final form will take. But whatever form, the experiences of the immigrant generation on the makeup and structure of American Jewry was immense and influential.

The Candles
of Shabbat

he tradition in Judaism of lighting Sabbath candles on
Friday night is an ancient one. It is of rabbinic origin
and is mentioned in the Mishnah and Talmud numerous times. It requires that the candles be lit eighteen to
twenty minutes before sunset on Friday night by the
woman of the house. It is one of the three special
mitzvot given over to the woman of the house to perform, the others being the observance of family purity
and the taking of "*challah*" (a small section) from the
dough of bread about to be baked. Usually a minimum
of two candles are lit, one in honor of the Sabbath commandment *zachor* — to remember the Sabbath day to
keep it holy; and the other candle represents *shamor* —
to guard the Sabbath by the non-performance of forbidden labors. These are the two statements regarding the
Sabbath that appear in the two texts of the Ten
Commandments in the Bible. And the two glowing candles symbolize our devotion to the Sabbath in these two

realms — one in the spiritual, intellectual sphere of remembering — *zachor* — and the other in the practical, physical sense — *shamor*, guarding the Sabbath from forbidden labors. Thus the two candles represent our commitment to the Creator, a commitment that the Sabbath itself represents.

Three main reasons are advanced for the lighting of the candles. The Sabbath requires that it be honored. Thus, the candles are lit in honor of the Sabbath. The candles are not the only sign of honor in the house for the Sabbath. The Talmud and Maimonides state that "beds should be made in order, and the table set properly for the Sabbath meal." The Sabbath is thus honored as a welcome and dear guest, a visit from a queen, so to speak. Royalty commands honor and respect. So does our Sabbath night and day.

A second reason for the lighting of candles is *oneg Shabbat* — the pleasure of the Sabbath. The prophet Isaiah enjoins us to "call the Sabbath pleasurable." Light is enjoyable. It enhances the ambiance of our home and provides a festive atmosphere for our meal. Light is the symbol of creation, as the first of God's creations. Light is also representative of Torah, as is stated in the Bible, "For a *mitzvah* is like a candle and Torah is light itself." The pleasures of the Sabbath are both physical and spiritual. Good food, family companionship, a relaxed atmosphere, sleep and rest, as well as the silenced telephone, radio and television, are all part of the physical enjoyments of the Sabbath. It is how we "call the Sabbath pleasurable." Torah study, synagogue attendance, meaningful reading and discussions are part of the spiritual side of the Sabbath's pleasures. The light of the candles represents the different types of joys and pleasures of the Sabbath as well. The Sabbath dispels the darkness of the everyday workweek and allows the light of our souls to shine forth.

The third reason for Sabbath candle lighting is *shalom bayit* — peace and contentment in the home. The light of the holy candles signifies the bond of marriage and family. The absence of the mundane requirements of the workweek allows time for healing and understanding, love and empathy. A dark house leads to depression and sadness. A house full of light restores cheerfulness, optimism and confident hope. Sabbath is a blanket of serenity in an otherwise turbulent world. It is a retreat to our inner place of peace and stability. Wars demand blackouts. Peace is always represented by light. Since the Sabbath is total peace, the lighting of candles is most appropriate. In the glow of the Sabbath candles we sense the fulfillment of another Biblical verse: "For in Your light, O God, shall we see light as well."

28 The Sabbath Table

One of the joys of the Sabbath is the appearance and décor of the table upon which the Sabbath meals are served. Sabbath meals are usually festive affairs, served in the dining room rather than the kitchen/breakfast nook where the rushed weekday meals are gobbled down. The Sabbath meal is leisurely, interspersed with song, discussions of Torah topics and other enjoyable and wholesome conversation. It is the venue for children to tell their families what they've learned that week at school. It also is the setting for hospitality to guests and friends and a time for family anecdotes, reminiscences and bonding. However, all emotional and spiritual experiences in this world require a physical framework.

The physical setting for the enhancement and release of the Sabbath meal's atmosphere is the Sabbath table itself. There is no more direct and telling lesson that can be taught to the members of the household about the importance of the Sabbath than the exhibition of the care and taste involved in preparing the Sabbath table. It is a labor of love, and different assignments regarding the table's preparation can and should be delegated to different members of the family. It is my personal experience with my children and grandchildren that those who are somewhat reluctant to share the burden of ordinary household chores are far more enthusiastic about fulfilling their obligations when it comes to setting the table for Sabbath.

The table is first covered with a Sabbath tablecloth. Such tablecloths are usually white, though they can be of any color. There are even special tablecloths with "Sabbath" embroidery or designs. The concept of a tablecloth is not only one of beauty and practicality. The Sabbath table, which has two loaves of *challah* (bread) placed on it, is a symbol of the miraculous manna that sustained the Hebrews during their forty-year sojourn in the Sinai Desert after the Exodus from Egypt. While on normal weekdays only one portion of manna fell for each individual, on Fridays two measures of manna fell in the desert, one measure for Friday and one for the Sabbath. This is the origin of having two loaves of *challah* on the table for the Sabbath meals. The manna that fell in the desert was sandwiched between two layers of dew that protected the manna from the sands below and the dust above it. Therefore, our custom is to sandwich the two loaves of *challah* between the tablecloth and a special cloth cover. The cover is usually decorated with "Sabbath" embroidery. Thus the tablecloth itself becomes a symbol of Jewish history and memory.

Before the meal, a goblet is placed on the table that will contain wine for the *Kiddush* blessing. This blessing refers to remembering the Sabbath as a gift to Israel by God and it sanctifies the meal about to be eaten. The goblet is usually made of silver, though almost any material can be used. The finest dishes, silverware and tableware are used for the Sabbath meals. In many homes, especially in Israel, flowers are placed on the table to add their flash of color. They also reflect the beauty of

God's world, created in six days before He "rested" on the seventh day, the Sabbath. And of course, the glow of candlelight on Friday night casts an atmosphere of spirituality over the entire scene.

The Sabbath table, therefore, is more than just a utilitarian table upon which food is placed and eaten. In the words of the prophets of Israel, the Sabbath table becomes "the table that is placed before the Lord." The Sabbath itself is an honored "guest," likened to a queen, in every Jewish home. Therefore, the table set before such an important and beloved guest must reflect the honor, happiness and satisfaction that the members of the household feel at entertaining such a guest in their home. In all of its beauty and dignity, the carefully set table speaks to us of the greatness and holiness of the Sabbath day itself.

29 **Sabbath Clothing**

O ne of the methods of sanctifying the Sabbath day and making it special, unique and different from the other days of the week is the wearing of Sabbath clothing. Jews traditionally wore special garments in honor of Sabbath. The origin of this custom is quite ancient, with Rashi and Midrash ascribing it to the time of the Judges (after the Hebrews settled the Land of Israel following their forty-year sojourn in the desert) and to the encounter of Ruth and Boaz. The Bible records that Ruth dressed carefully and specially for the occasion, and the rabbis interpreted that to mean that she wore her special Sabbath clothing. Throughout the ages, the form, color and style of Sabbath clothing may have changed, but the basic concept of honoring the Sabbath with special garb has remained constant. Even among the poorest of Jewish families, some designated Sabbath wear was the norm.

Currently, in our more affluent times, Sabbath clothing has taken on a new and relatively more luxurious dimension. In Chassidic circles, a long coat (usually black in color) of satin and brocade, together with an expensive fur hat (*shtreimel*) are common male Sabbath clothing. The fur hats are copies of the types of headgear worn in the eighteenth century by Polish and Russian nobility. Some decades ago, when there still was a Soviet Union, there was an exhibit in New York titled "Treasures From the Kremlin." Among the items displayed was the fur hat of Peter the Great. It is identical to the *shtreimel* worn by many, if not most, Chassidic Jews on Sabbath and holidays today. But Peter's hat had a gold cross on top.

Non-Chassidic men wear dress suits, or Prince Albert frocks. In Israel, the custom of Ashkenazic men in Jerusalem is to wear silver or white robes on the Sabbath, while Sephardic Jews wear white garments according to the tradition of the great sixteenth century mentor of *Kabbalah*, Rabbi Isaac Luria Ashkenazi (Ari). White shirts are commonly worn in honor of the Sabbath. Whatever the garb, the unifying factor is that millions of Jews wear some special type of clothing in order to mark the holy Sabbath day.

Women have much greater variety in their choice of Sabbath garments. Again, the unifying factor is that the garments worn are of best quality and fit the category of being "dressed up." Children also are provided with special Sabbath clothes. I remember fondly and with great nostalgia how my children, when they were yet young and small, would speak about their new shoes as "Shabbos shoes."

Wearing new clothing for the first time is also usually reserved for the Sabbath day or for holidays. The tradition of special clothing for holidays is even stronger than the one for Sabbath clothing. Sabbath clothing is worn for all special family occasions, as well for important communal events. It is a sign of respect for the event to wear one's Sabbath clothing.

In 1882, the great Rabbi Naftali Zvi Yehuda Berlin, the head of the nineteenth century Yeshivah of Volozhin and an ardent lover of the Land of Israel, wore his Sabbath garments in honor of the delivery of a bottle of wine from Baron Rothschild's Carmel

Wineries in Rishon Letziyon, Palestine! Many Jews wore their Sabbath clothing on the day that they were privileged to reach the shores of the Land of Israel.

Thus, Sabbath clothing signifies more than just cloth, leather and fur. Sabbath clothing became the external symbol of the internal holiness of time, space and the soul of the Jewish People throughout the ages.

30 The Day of Rest

The day that defines the Jewish calendar, and therefore Jews themselves, is the Sabbath — the day of rest that comes every Friday night and Saturday. The concept of a day of rest every week is one of the major contributions of Judaism to world civilization. Jewish tradition teaches us that even in Egypt the Jews were granted a day of rest on the Sabbath day.

According to Jewish tradition, the laws and concepts of the Sabbath day were taught to the Children of Israel in the desert at the oasis of Marah, even before the revelation at Sinai (the giving of the Torah to the nation) took place. The commandment to remember and observe the Sabbath is the fourth of the Ten Commandments and it is the one commandment that has more words and explanation to it than any other of the Ten Commandments. The emphasis on Sabbath observance, repeated so often in the Torah, became the foundation of Jewish life and society throughout the ages. In Jewish law, it became the fault line of Jewish behavior and the determining factor of legal Jewish status regarding trustworthiness, loyalty to God and other matters. "Sabbath observer" became the proud definition of a Jew.

The day of rest, as defined by Jewish law and custom, consists of abstention from "work." Many people are under the misconception that forbidden "work" is labor. In this context, "work" is a difficult term to define. The Talmud devoted one of its largest volumes to detailing and explaining the concept of "work" as it relates to the Sabbath day. The Talmud defines as work any type of physical activity that was employed in the construction, maintenance or transportation of the Tabernacle that the Jews built in the Sinai Desert. In prohibiting these activities on the Sabbath, the message to the nation was that although the building of this important and sacred portable Temple was the key project of their lives, the keeping of the Lord's day of rest was even more essential to their spiritual and physical survival. If God saw fit to suspend the building of this central institution of Judaism on the Sabbath, it would be wrong to "honor" God by transgressing His law.

What types of activity are prohibited? The Talmud categorizes thirty-nine types of "work" that went into the Tabernacle project. These include agricultural work, actual construction tasks, work related to animals and food preparation, writing, sewing and many other types of human activity. Not all forbidden Sabbath labor need necessarily be physically strenuous, just as not all physically taxing effort is in itself forbidden on the Sabbath. The measuring rod is whether the labor and/or effort falls into any one of the thirty-nine categories defined as "work" by the Talmud. For example, carrying objects inside an enclosed area was not part of the Tabernacle categories of work, while carrying outside in a public domain was. This is why carrying a heavy object within one's home is permissible while carrying even a key or a handkerchief in a public locale is forbidden where there is no halachic (legal according to Jewish law) eiruv present. An eiruv is a halachically recognized "fence" or barrier that encloses a public area and thereby transforms it into a private area, allowing for the carrying of objects in that space on the Sabbath. Most major Jewish communities in the world have constructed such an *eiruv* in the Jewish neighborhoods of their cities. In Israel, all cities and towns have an *eiruv*.

The Talmud also explains that the results of forbidden "work" — such as a burning fire — are permissible if the actual "work" of lighting the fire was accomplished before the onset of the Sabbath and the fire continues to burn by itself on the Sabbath. This concept of "automatic work" lies at the heart of many of the devices used by Jews today to make their Sabbath day more comfortable. Special devices such as timer clocks that are set before the Sabbath and which then control lighting, air conditioning, etc. on the Sabbath day are much in vogue in the Jewish world today. There are also computer devices that control elevators on the Sabbath. These devices are common in almost all hotels and many private apartment buildings throughout the State of Israel. There is an enormous amount of rabbinic literature dealing with modern technology and our ancient categories of Sabbath "work."

31 Havdalah

The ceremony that concludes the Sabbath day, as well as the holidays of the year, is called *Havdalah* — literally meaning separation. This ceremony signifies Judaism's message that not everything is equal, as far as spiritual matters are concerned. One of the glaring weaknesses of current Western society and politics is its tendency towards moral equivalency. There is no standard of right and wrong, good and bad, justified behavior and unwarranted actions present in much of our modern world. This absence of differences flies in the face of Jewish traditional values that are careful to delineate levels of morality, goodness and holiness. This ability to separate and delineate, to judge carefully and recognize differences lies at the basis of Judaic practice, ritual, Torah study and worldview. And it is the *Havdalah* ceremony that most clearly illustrates this facet of Jewish thought and behavior.

The ceremony contains a text that expresses this idea simply and completely. It remarks upon the difference between light and dark; between the holy and the profane; between the sanctity of the Sabbath day and the days of the workaday week. It also refers to the uniqueness of the Jewish people and acknowledges the concomitant uniqueness of the covenant that binds Israel to its God. It strengthens the idea of the Shabbat by separating it from the other days of the week. It emphasizes its special status as the basis of the Jewish concepts of time and of God as the Creator of the universe.

This understanding of the Sabbath day as the center point of Jewish time and as the source of the holiness of time is further reinforced by the inclusion in the *Havdalah* service of the ritual of smelling sweet spices in order to "restore our souls." The Jewish tradition is that on the Sabbath each of us receives an extra measure of spirituality and sanctity — "an extra soul." When the Sabbath departs, so does this "extra soul." To alleviate this sense of loss (which I can personally attest is palpable) the rabbis initiated the custom of introducing the sweet fragrance of spices into the *Havdalah* service.

As with many other Jewish rituals, *Havdalah* blessings are conducted over a cup of wine. Wine is a drink of importance in Jewish tradition and therefore lends an aura of solemnity and importance to the accompanying ritual.

Another custom that forms part of the service is the blessing of thanks for fire. This blessing is recited over a multi-wicked candle commonly marketed specifically as a *Havdalah* candle. This multi-wicked candle is currently available in a great variety of shapes and colors and has lately become the object of much creative artistry, especially in Israel. Jewish legend tells us that the invention of fire by man, the basic requirement for any sort of technical progress in civilization, occurred on the night after the first Sabbath. Thus the *Havdalah* candle also symbolizes man's unending and innate drive to create, invent and attempt to make life physically more comfortable. As such, it serves as the proper introduction to the week of work and labor that follows the end of the Sabbath day. It is the harbinger of the "good week" to come.

The traditional Jewish greeting one to another on Saturday night is "Good Week/*Shavuah Tov* (Hebrew) or *Gut Voch* (Yiddish)." Thus, the two Jewish greetings for the week's events reflect the Jew's daily reality: either "Good Sabbath/*Shabbat Shalom*" or "*Shavuah Tov*/Good Week." And in reality that pretty much sums up the cycle of the week, if not of Jewish life itself.

Holidays and
Special Days

*T*he Jewish year is regularly marked with days
of holiness and commemoration. The festiveness
of the Jewish holidays differs in nature from the
special serenity of the Sabbath. Some types of "work"
which are forbidden on the Sabbath are permitted on
the holidays, especially regarding the preparation
of food. Sumptuous meals are served and the finest
clothing is worn on the holidays, even more so than
on the Sabbath. The holidays are a time for family,
friends, visits, songs, festive synagogue services, Torah
lectures and a complete emotional break from the
tensions and problems of everyday life.

The three main Biblical festivals are Passover, at
the beginning of the spring season, Shavuot in early
summer and Succot early in the autumn. In ancient
times, Jews from all over Israel would "go up" to
Jerusalem for the Holy Temple services of these
holidays. The rabbinic festivals (instituted to celebrate
specific miracles many years after the giving of the
Torah) are Chanukah, in the middle of the winter,
and Purim at the end of that season. The High
Holy Days of Rosh Hashanah and Yom Kippur have
a flavor all their own, a combination of spiritual
exhilaration and solemnity.

There also four rabbinic fast days observed in
addition to the great Biblical fast of repentance on

Yom Kippur. Other days of remembrance and historical tradition are interspersed throughout the year as well. In short, the cycle of the Jewish calendar year encompasses all of the ideas, tenets, traditions and customs of Israel and in itself is truly representative of the faith of Judaism, its goals and beliefs.

This chapter provides a cursory view of this Jewish year cycle and of the special days that mark its unending movement. These special days mark points of reference in our own personal journey through life. They are the buoys in the channel that mark the entrance to the safe harbor of God's presence and guidance in our often storm-tossed waters of life.

32 Measuring Time

n our modern world, it seems that everyone has at least one watch. There are millions of watches sold every year, ranging from those that cost less than ten dollars to tens of thousands of dollars. Today, watches are not only instruments that measure the passing of time but also represent fashion and status. We are so accustomed to watches, clocks and instruments that can measure time to a thousandth of a second it is difficult to imagine that such instruments are a relatively late invention. Knowing the exact time is more than a convenience. In some cultures, it is crucial. What is the importance of telling time in Jewish tradition?

The Jewish day is built on sunset, the appearance of night stars, the morning star, dawn and sunrise. The time for the morning service begins with the morning star/dawn and continues for approximately a third of the day. There is a special merit in the morning services being recited exactly at sunrise, fulfilling the promise of the verse that "You [God] will be seen with the first rays of the sun." Since exact times could not be identified before watches, the physical signs of sunrise, sunset, etc. were and are employed in Jewish law to determine times of prayer. The afternoon service should take place after half of the day has gone and before the sun has set, and the evening service takes place after sunset, preferably when the night stars have become visible.

Sunrise and sunset (besides being the words to a once-popular song) are also the determining factors of the entry and exit times of the Sabbath and Jewish holy days. The Sabbath arrives eighteen minutes before sunset and it ends approximately forty-five minutes after sunset for most Jews in America and Israel. Customs vary on the ending time of the Sabbath and there are many Jews the world over who wait seventy-two minutes after sunset. Before watches, these times were approximations, depending on the expertise of those analyzing the late afternoon and night skies.

There are also set times for the recitation of the *Shema* ("Hear O Israel, the Lord is our God, the Lord is One."), the basic prayer and statement of the Jewish faith. It may be said until a third of the day has passed. There is a difference of Jewish legal opinion as to whether the day is to be measured from sunrise to sunset or from dawn until the appearance of the night stars, which gives rise to differing observances. This difference of opinion also comes into play on the eve of Passover, when eating *chametz* (leavened bread) is forbidden after a third of the day passes. The "burning of the *chametz*" should occur within the next hour, so again time is critical.

Midnight also played a role in Jewish tradition. Jews would rise (some still do) at midnight to recite prayers of longing and devotion regarding Jerusalem and the Land of Israel, and to mourn for the destroyed Temple and the spiritual benefits the Jews have lost due to its destruction. This custom was called *Tikkun Chatzot* — literally, the "order of prayer for midnight." Here the time need not be as exact as the other instances mentioned above, though the kabbalists always attempted to recite these prayers as close to exact midnight as possible, as they were of the opinion that the gates of heaven were then especially open for receiving prayer and supplication.

The Jewish calendar is basically a lunar one. In order to balance a shorter 354-day lunar year with the longer 365-day solar calendar, the Jewish calendar is arranged in nineteen-year cycles, with seven 13-month years and twelve 12-month years included in each cyle. Every Jewish month begins with a one- or two-day commemoration called Rosh Chodesh — "the beginning of the new month." The Rosh Chodesh day or days is a minor holiday, for Rosh Chodesh is symbolic of the renewal of the Jewish People that is represented by the renewal of the new moon.

Though the instruments for measuring time have changed and developed over the centuries, the measurement of time was always woven into Jewish life. The daily pattern of Jewish existence has always revolved around it, keeping the Jew forever aware of the movements of the sun and moon in the universe, and underscoring his relationship to this orderly and harmonious aspect of Creation.

The Names of
33 Jewish Months

The Jewish calendar is based on both lunar and solar cycles. It provides for a year of twelve months that constitute 354 days, corresponding to a lunar year. Seven times in a nineteen-year cycle the year contains thirteen months; the resulting year can stretch to 384 (sometimes 385) days. But this chapter is not about the machinations and calculations of the Hebrew calendar itself. Rather, I wish to discuss the "Hebrew" names given to the months of the calendar year.

In the Bible we find that the months of the year were given purely numerical names. Passover is to fall on the fifteenth day of the "first" month; Rosh Hashanah is to be the first day of the "seventh" month and so on. The Torah tell us that the revelation at Sinai occurred in the "third" month and all of the other historical references in the Torah — the dedication of the Tabernacle, the beginning date of Moses' final words to Israel, etc.— are identified by numbered months. The month of the onset of spring was identified as being the "head" or "first" month, and all of the other months and their numbered names were based on that description.

However, we find in later Biblical books that Hebrew names were given to some of the months of the year. In the Book of Kings we read that the "second" month was called *Ziv*. This Hebrew word, which loosely translated means splendor, fit the "second" month because of the beauty of nature and the comfortable climate that occurs during that month in the Land of Israel. The "seventh" month also came to be called by the specific Hebrew name *Eitanim*. This name denotes great stature and strength and fits that month because of the holidays that occur then — Rosh Hashanah, Yom Kippur and Succot — and also because it is the month of the birth of the great founding patriarchs of the Jewish People. Yet, throughout the period of the Prophets and the time of the First Temple, the use of numbered names of the calendar months persisted and was the accepted norm.

All of this changed with the return of the Jewish People from the Babylonian exile with Ezra the Scribe, at the beginning of the Second Temple era. The Talmud records for us that "the names of the months of the Hebrew calendar came up to the Land of Israel with the returning Jews from Babylonia." These names were not necessarily Hebrew in origin. For example, Tamuz is a particularly strange name for a Jewish month, since in the Bible it is identified as the name of a pagan deity. Nevertheless, these Babylonian month names have stuck with us even to this present day. Their use by the Jewish People for well over two millennia has hallowed them so that there is no hesitation in their use despite their non-Jewish origin. I would venture to say that most Jews are not even aware that these names are Babylonian and not Hebrew. Ever since the Babylonian exile, then, our calendar names for the months from "first" to "twelfth" are: Nissan, Iyar, Sivan, Tamuz, Av, Elul, Tishrei, MarCheshvan, Kislev, Tevet, Shevat and Adar. In a leap year of thirteen months, the thirteenth month is called "Second Adar."

Many explanations have been advanced as to why the Jews chose and kept these names for their calendar months. The retention of the Babylonian language for the names of the months may be due to the everlasting prominence of the Babylonian Jewish community and the leadership role that it played in the Jewish world for more than a thousand years. But the true reason behind this interesting anomaly in Jewish life still remains shrouded in mystery and is a ready subject for scholarly research.

34 Rosh Hashanah

The advent of the Jewish New Year is marked by the holiday of Rosh Hashanah. This holiday is many faceted and complex — a puzzling combination of somber solemnity and of pleasant confidence, new clothes, sumptuous meals and holiday enjoyment. In reconciling these completely different emotions and aspects of the holiday, the rabbis relied on the sophistication and maturity of the Jewish People. In truth, all of Jewish history and life require the ability to deal with somber events and an uncertain future with aplomb, hope and a resilient spirit of optimism. Therefore, Rosh Hashanah not only symbolizes the beginning of a new year on the Jewish calendar, it represents the beginning *idea* of Judaism and its tradition — the ability to reconcile opposite emotions and events and to remain faithful and upbeat about life and its possibilities. Judaism teaches, above all else, the sense of service to God and humankind that foster confidence and serenity within us, despite pressures and threats.

Rosh Hashanah is a day of judgment. It is this aspect of the holiday that engenders its somber tone. The Mishnah describes how on Rosh Hashanah, each individual human soul files by the Heavenly Throne for judgment. This serious event is reflected in the somber mood of the prayers of the day and pleading quality of the melodies used by the leader of the services. In these special prayers, the sovereignty of God over the entire world is acknowledged and contemplated. Much of the service is, in a sense, a coronation — proclaiming God's kingdom anew.

The most exalted set of prayers recited in the *Musaf* service of Rosh Hashanah consists of three sections. They are called:

Malchiyot (relating to the majesty of God);

Zichronot (relating to the role of memory and history in positively influencing our ultimate judgment at the heavenly trial); and

Shofrot (relating to the sounding of the *shofar*), which is the unique *mitzvah* (commandment) of Rosh Hashanah.

The text of the prayers in use today in most synagogues was written by the great second century Babylonian Talmudic scholar and leader, Rabbi Abba Aricha — more commonly known in the Talmud as Rav ("The Rabbi"/teacher). These prayers have stood the test of nineteen centuries, and millions of Jewish tears have been shed while reciting them over the ages. They are unmatched for linguistic beauty, clarity of thought and nobility of soul. Even in translation to other languages from the original Hebrew, their holiness and shimmering light is readily detected.

The most dramatic moment of the holiday is the sounding of the *shofar*. It is usually made of a ram's horn, though that of an ibex or similar animal may also be used. There are three basic notes that are sounded from the *shofar*. One is a straight, flat tone called *tekiah*. The second note consists of three wailing blasts of sound: It is called *shevarim*. The third type of sound is a staccato of nine short blasts, called *teruah*. The wailing and staccato sounds are always preceded by the straight, flat sound. The flat sound suggests our mortality and limited lifespan, much as a heart monitor does when it goes flat, marking the end of a life. The wailing and staccato sounds, reminiscent of human sobbing and longing, mark the turbulence of our lives, our strivings, ambitions and goals, while we are alive. The flat sound therefore precedes and succeeds the wailing and staccato sounds, for it symbolizes our state of existence before our birth and after our passing. The Biblical injunction of "sounding the *shofar*" is accomplished by sounding thirty blasts from the *shofar*. However it is ancient Jewish custom to sound one hundred blasts from the *shofar*.

Because the *shofar* is usually fashioned from a ram's horn, it is inextricably linked to the Biblical story of the binding of Isaac by his father, Abraham, on the sacrificial altar. Once it was clear that both father and son were prepared to follow God's directive, no matter how much it ran counter to their earlier concepts of His Will, God rescinded His order and a ram was sacrificed in Isaac's stead. Jewish legend states that one of the horns of that ram was sounded on Mt. Sinai when Israel received God's Torah and that the second horn of that ram will be sounded to introduce the Messianic Era. In this light, we see Rosh Hashanah as encompassing past, present and future, in both solemnity and joy.

35 New Year's Greetings

t is customary, and certainly most understandable and desirable, that Jews wish each other a happy new year prior to and on the holiday of Rosh Hashanah. This custom is enshrined in Jewish law, for it is mentioned in all legal references to the holiday of Rosh Hashanah. In fact, the *halachah* (Jewish law) states that during the entire month of Elul, the Hebrew month that precedes Rosh Hashanah, one should be scrupulous when writing a letter to an acquaintance to include in the salutation or conclusion the warmest wishes for a good new year. Because of this halachic requirement of courtesy and felicity, it became customary throughout Jewish history for Jews to write letters of New Year's greetings to family, friends and acquaintances, even if the letter had no other purpose than the greeting itself.

One of the inventions of nineteenth century Western civilization was the greeting card. The non-Jewish world used greeting cards to extend kind wishes on Christmas.

Christmas and Christian New Year cards rapidly grew into a major industry, with millions being printed and sold annually. The Jewish world adopted and adapted this type of greeting card for its own purposes during the Rosh Hashanah season. By the end of the nineteenth century, Jewish New Year cards were all the rage. Many prominent religious, social and political leaders had their own custom-made greeting cards printed. Some individuals had a family photograph made into a New Year's greeting card and then sent these pictures to their relatives who lived far away from them. This was especially true of Jewish immigrants to America who still had many relatives residing in Eastern Europe. Most other Jews purchased ready-made cards that were printed and distributed in the hundreds of thousands. In the twentieth century, all of the major greeting card firms in the United States produced greeting cards for the Jewish New Year in great variety and number.

The Jewish greeting card was also used extensively by various Jewish organizations and ideologies as a method of spreading and promulgating their policies and opinions. The Zionist movement made extensive use of picture greeting cards to get across its message for the return of the Jewish People to the ancient homeland of Israel. Pictures of Herzl, of Zionist congresses and leaders, of kibbutzim and young Jewish farmers tilling the soil of the Land of Israel were commonly used for this purpose. Even secular, Leftist and openly anti-religious Jewish organizations such as the Jewish Labor Union/Bund distributed many thousands of Jewish New Year's cards to its members and to other Jews. These cards naturally expressed the hope that the coming year would bring about the triumph and solidarity of the laboring class and the utopian rule of the proletariat. The irony of sending Rosh Hashanah cards, celebrating a religious holiday that these very organizations would deny existence in their future workers' paradise, was apparently lost on them.

The use of printed and posted greeting cards has declined in the past few decades, both in the Jewish and non-Jewish world. The telephone, fax, e-mail and other modern conveniences of communication have undermined the role and necessity of the old-fashioned greeting card. We also live in a time of lessened gentility and courtesy, where manners and societal conventions no longer hold the powerful sway on people that they did previously.

Nevertheless, the traditional advice to wish one's fellow Jew good fortune in the coming year should not be forgotten or discarded. Our sages have taught us that sincerely expressed good wishes extended to others rebound to the benefit of the one giving the blessing. Those who bless others are always blessed themselves.

36 Apples and Honey

All Jewish customs have Torah, historical and traditional origins, though many of them may be somewhat obscure due to the passage of time and the circumstances of the long exile of the People of Israel. Why is an apple dipped in honey at the start of the Jewish New Year? What is the special symbolism of the apple that makes it the fruit that most often graces our Rosh Hashanah table?

The sophisticated doubters among us have stated that the apple is used because it is the fruit that was most available in all of the areas of the world of the Jewish Exile. However, such reasoning begs the question and misses the entire point of the reasons for the preservation of Jewish customs. Jewish customs reinforce Jewish identity and memory. They serve to remind us of our special responsibility and duties towards God and man. They reinforce our sense of solidarity with all of the previous Jewish generations and provide an effective method of transmitting our tradition and heritage to our children and grandchildren.

The custom of eating an apple dipped into honey on the night of Rosh Hashanah does have a special traditional significance. Its origins enhance the beauty and sweetness of the custom. One of the fruits to which the Jewish People are compared in King Solomon's allegorical *Song of Songs* is the apple. "As the apple is rare and unique among the trees of the forest, so is my beloved [Israel] among the maidens [nations] of the world." The Midrash informs us that the apple tree puts forth the nub of its fruit even before the leaves that will surround and protect the little fruit at its beginning stage of growth are fully sprouting. The Jewish People, by accepting the Torah with the statement, "We will do and we will understand" — placing holy action and observance of Torah commandments even before understanding and rational acceptance — thereby imitated this characteristic of the apple. Thus, the apple became a Jewish symbol, a memory aid of sorts, of the moment of revelation at Sinai.

The apple also serves to remind the Jewish People of their enslavement in Egypt and their deliverance from that bondage. Again, according to Midrash, the apple served as the fruit of affection between husband and wife during the long and painful period of abject slavery. It provided them with hope and determination to bring a future generation into the world despite all of the bleakness of their Jewish circumstance. The apple therefore also became the symbol of the Jewish home and family, of optimism and of a brighter Jewish future, of the tenacity of Jewish spirit and determination.

It is interesting to note that in general society, the apple is assigned the role of the fruit of temptation in the Biblical story of Adam and Eve in the Garden of Eden. In the non-Jewish world, the apple therefore became the symbol of human weakness and downfall, even of death itself. However, when the Talmud lists the possible "fruits" that may have been the product of the Tree of Knowledge in the Garden of Eden it does not include apples. The "fruits" mentioned are wheat, figs and grapes.

There is one Jewish source for an apple being that fateful fruit, quoted in Midrash, but it does not have the weight of authority that a Talmudic statement possesses. The Christian world, for unknown reasons, adopted the view of that Midrash and all Christian art, story and religious tradition for the last 1,500 years has given the apple a bad name.

Not so among Jews, where the apple retains its positive symbolism and has its place of honor on our Rosh Hashanah table as a harbinger of a good, sweet and holy year for us all.

THE SIGNIFICANCE OF HONEY

Traditionally, from Rosh Hashanah until after the holiday of Succot, honey is served with every major meal and is an ingredient in dozens of foods. It is smeared on the bread over which we recite the *Hamotzi* blessing. A sweet apple is dipped into honey on the night of Rosh Hashanah, baked goods are made with honey, and honey is used in the preparation of foods such as glazed carrots and sweet desserts. Aside from the caloric disaster that this custom entails, one is really hard pressed to find a negative thing to say about honey.

Putting honey on the Jewish table during this holiday time period is an ancient and universal Jewish custom. It is recorded in the works of the Babylonian Geonim of the seventh century and probably dates back to even much earlier times. It is no exaggeration to say that Jews always seemed to possess a sweet tooth.

The obvious reason for the use of honey on our table at this time of the year is the symbolism of our desire for a sweet new year. "Sweet" means dear, precious, enjoyable, satisfying, serene, secure and something most pleasing. That about sums up our hopes and prayers for the coming year and therefore honey serves as our representative in expressing these fervent hopes and prayers.

Yet honey represents more than sweetness per se. It is one of the attributes of the Land of Israel, which is described in the Bible as being a land that "flows with milk and honey." Thus honey on the table always reminded the Jews, wherever they resided, of their ancient homeland of Israel and of the Jewish attachment to its history and holy soil. In actuality, the honey referred to in the expression of "a land flowing with milk and honey" is not the common bee honey that we use today, but describes rather the honey of Biblical times that was primarily produced from dates. Even today, date honey is produced and sold in Israel, though the overwhelming majority of honey used comes from bees.

The use of bee honey as a permissible kosher food raises an interesting question of Jewish law. The general rule is that food products that are derived from non-kosher creatures are never considered to be kosher for Jewish use as a food. Bees are a non-kosher species of insect life and therefore one would think that the honey that they produce within the sacs of their bodies would also not be kosher. Yet in the Bible we find reference to the use of honey as a food.

Why is this different from, let us say, milk from a camel that remains non-kosher, since the camel itself which gave the milk is a non-kosher animal? The rabbis of the Talmud studied the problem and found that the sac in the bee containing the honey is only a storage place for the honey and neither it or the honey produced are an integral part of the bee's body, whereas the milk-producing organs and the lactating process of the camel are an integral part of the camel's circulatory and digestive system and thus the camel and its milk both have the same legal status of being non-kosher.

Its symbolism of sweetness in life, its connection to the Land of Israel, its role in halachic (Jewish legal) discussion concerning its *kashrut,* all have combined to make honey a "Jewish" food for centuries. Its use is certainly one of the sweetest customs of Jewish tradition.

37 **Tashlich**

O ne of the most popular and unique customs of the holy day of Rosh Hashanah is the recitation of the prayer called *Tashlich*. That Hebrew word's literal meaning is "to cast away." The custom and the word are derived from a verse in the book of the prophet Micah that states: "[God] will return and bestow His mercy upon us, hide our sins and cast away in the depths of the sea our transgressions." Based on that verse, a custom arose over the centuries that on the afternoon of the first day of Rosh Hashanah Jews go to a body of water, there "to cast away" their sins. This symbolic act represents the beginning of the Ten Days of Repentance from Rosh Hashanah through Yom Kippur and signifies our commitment to abandon wrongful behavior in the coming year.

Over the years, *Tashlich* became a custom of social and community behavior. I remember that as a small child I sat on my grandfather's front porch on Douglas Boulevard in Chicago, and I watched tens of thousands of

Jews in that heavily Jewish neighborhood walking in their holiday finery to the Douglas Park lagoon to say *Tashlich*. It was such a notable event that the newspapers in Chicago regularly printed articles and pictures describing the gathering. As is obvious, going to *Tashlich* took on a social connotation and was no longer a purely religious act. Because of this, some rabbis criticized the custom, stating that the socializing aspect of *Tashlich* negated its original holy symbolic purpose.

Yet the custom flourished and is observed throughout the Jewish world today. To avoid the socializing problem, many perform the custom of *Tashlich* during the week between Rosh Hashanah and Yom Kippur, when attendance at the body of water is usually sparse.

At *Tashlich*, certain parts of the Bible, especially from Psalms, are recited. Prayers for health, prosperity, children and peace have also been inserted in the *Tashlich* service. The service concludes with the verse from the prophet Micah quoted above.

Some Jews also turn their pockets inside out, to symbolize that they carry away no residue of sin or evil behavior after the service. Because the custom was to go to bodies of water that contained fish — their eyes are always open to look heavenward — for the *Tashlich* service, children often bring along crumbs to feed the fish. This makes *Tashlich* a family event. The thrust of all Jewish religious customs has always been to involve our children in order to implant within them the traditions, values and lifestyle of Judaism.

The attachment of the Jewish People to the custom of *Tashlich* is so strong that even in communities that do not contain bodies of water — such as Jerusalem — the custom is still celebrated, albeit over "bodies of water" which require some imagination. Nevertheless, the symbolism of the custom still survives, and I find it to be very comforting in a difficult and profane world. It is not easy to cast away sin, but the concept of transforming our spiritual being is a powerful one. *Tashlich* is a custom that points the way in that most positive direction. It gives us pause and allows us to focus on self-improvement. Like all Jewish customs, it should therefore be appreciated, treasured and observed.

38 Shabbat Shuvah

The Sabbath that falls between Rosh Hashanah and Yom Kippur, the period of penitential thought and time in the Jewish calendar year, is Shabbat Shuvah. On this Sabbath a special *haftorah*, a reading from the prophets Hoshea, Yoel and Micah, is recited in the synagogue service. This *haftorah* begins with the Hebrew word *shuvah* — return! This fact contributes to a similar special name of this Sabbath as the Sabbath of Repentance (Shabbat Teshuvah), i.e. the return of every individual Jew to God and His Torah. It is one of the two designated "special" Sabbaths of the year. The other one is the Sabbath that precedes the holiday of Passover and is called Shabbat Hagadol — the Great Sabbath.

Throughout much of Jewish history, community rabbis were valued much more for their scholarship, their ability to decide matters of Jewish law and their human relations talents than for their oratorical skills. For example, in Eastern European Jewish society, rabbis hardly ever spoke publicly to their congregations nor did they deliver weekly sermons. The role of public speaker was filled by the *maggid*, usually an itinerant speaker who journeyed from place to place to deliver words of comfort, inspiration, chastisement and wisdom. The arrival of the *maggid* in town was an event! People closed their shops, quit their work and flocked to the town's synagogue to hear his words. The typical *maggid* spoke in a sing-song manner, with a melody that constantly changed to fit the varying themes of his speech. He called forth laughter at his witticisms and tears at his portrayal of human pathos and pain. And he always wove a Torah theme into his speech.

In larger communities such as Vilna, the *maggid* was a person of note who delivered regular, if not weekly, Torah discourses. As such, he was considered to be the "speaking" rabbi while the actual rabbi of the community was the scholar and spiritual leader of the local Jewish society.

However, the communal rabbi was obligated by custom and tradition, dating back to Talmudic times, to deliver two major sermons during the year: one on Shabbat Hagadol and another on Shabbat Shuvah. The lecture on Shabbat Hagadol almost always dealt with laws and customs pertaining to Passover, and included material regarding the Exodus from Egypt and the Torah's definition of individual and national freedom.

The address on Shabbat Shuvah concentrated on the ideas of repentance, self-analysis and personal improvement as well as a discussion of the pertinent laws regarding the observance of the Yom Kippur fast day. These two speeches were also a showcase for the rabbi's erudition and scholarship and each was usually a two-hour affair, if not longer.

The rabbinic speech on Shabbat Shuvah is still alive and well in the Jewish world today. Though today's communal rabbis usually speak or deliver a formal sermon on every Shabbat of the year, there still is a special aura about the lecture on Shabbat Shuvah. Rabbis no longer speak for two hours, but it is certainly not unusual for the sermon to last an hour. It still is composed of a mixture of *halachah* — Torah laws — and *aggadah* — homiletical insights and stories.

The Shabbat Shuvah address affords the rabbi and his congregants a special moment of bonding, understanding and appreciation for one another. It is therefore seen as part of the *teshuvah* (repentance) process of returning to spirituality. As a rabbi who has delivered a Shabbat Shuvah sermon every year for more than forty-five years, I can attest to the uniqueness, emotion and inspiration of the experience.

39 Yom Kippur

Yom Kippur is the holiest day of the Jewish calendar. It is a day of abstention, of prayer and meditation, of introspection, of soul-searching and repentance. It is called the "Sabbath of Sabbaths" — the ultimate day of spirit and serenity. Jews dress in white as a sign of purity and as a reminder of our mortality, for ultimately we are buried in white shrouds. Men usually wear a white robe called a *kittel* and a white *yarmulke* (skullcap) during the synagogue service; women wear white clothing and do not wear jewelry.

The white garments are also a reminder of the vestment the *Kohen Gadol*, the High Priest, wore on Yom Kippur during most of the Yom Kippur service in the Holy Temple in Jerusalem. He donned four plain white garments — shirt, pants, sash and hat — without the four gold garments — the long coat, breastplate, head ornament and apron — that he ordinarily wore in performing his Temple duties. The gold garments are not worn on this day of asking forgiveness because they represent human pride and majesty and are a potential reminder of the sin of the Golden Calf. Yom Kippur is a day of humility. Fancy garments, especially gold garments, are out of place and contrary to the prevailing spirit of this holy day.

On Yom Kippur, Jews abstain from doing any work, from eating and drinking, from marital relations, from wearing leather shoes and from washing. Maimonides classifies these abstentions as being forms of "rest" for this Sabbath of Sabbaths. We rest from the world and our ordinary necessities on this day. The day is marked with this atmosphere of serenity, coupled with a seriousness of purpose, though not with any tinge of sadness. On this day, with God's mercy, our sins are erased and forgiven, and thus it is an occasion of joy and not one of sadness.

We confess our sins in the prayer services of Yom Kippur nine times (including the afternoon *Minchah* prayer before Yom Kippur) and we beseech God's understanding of our frailties and weaknesses. We also pledge to try to improve and to become better Jews and finer human beings. All of these confessions refer only to sins between ourselves and our Creator. It is within the power of Yom Kippur to absolve these transgressions. However, sins that were committed against our fellow human beings are not absolved by Yom Kippur. They can be erased only when the wronged party forgives our acts or statements. Thus, before Yom Kippur we seek out those whom we may have possibly wronged during the course of the year, and we request their understanding and forgiveness. It is wrong for a Jew to withhold such forgiveness if sincerely asked for it. Only if we are willing to forgive each other can we then in good conscience ask God to forgive our sins as well.

The enemies of Israel always marked Yom Kippur as a special day of hatred towards the Jews. From the execution of Rabbi Akiva by the Romans on Yom Kippur in Caesarea in 139 CE, through the Holocaust and the Israeli Yom Kippur War of 1973, Yom Kippur carries stark memories for the Jewish People. These memories have been woven into the prayers of the day.

The *Kol Nidrei* prayer that introduces the prayer services on Yom Kippur eve has such overtones. Though it existed prior to the fifteenth century, it took on special importance to the Jewish *conversos* of Spain, who had been forced to renounce Judaism and convert to Christianity. This prayer nullifies false vows and coerced undertakings and allows all of Israel, sinners and saints, to pray in the congregation as one.

There is perhaps no other day on the Jewish calendar that so unifies the Jewish People as Yom Kippur. It creates social amity, fosters the repairing of relationships between human beings, renews commitment to God and deepens our sense of personal connection with generations past and future. Yom Kippur is the quintessential Jewish day, unmatched by any other faith or nation in the world.

40 The Joy of Succot

Passover is the holiday of freedom, Shavuot is the holiday of receiving the Torah, but only Succot is singled out as the holiday of emotion — of joy. A Biblical harvest festival, Succot notably commemorates the encampment of our ancestors in the Sinai Desert for forty years under the protective clouds of God's presence. Why does the Torah refer to it as "the time of joy"?

Succot comes a few days after Yom Kippur — in many ways it is the culmination of the Rosh Hashanah/Yom Kippur experience — and the knowledge that we have been granted forgiveness is a source of great joy. The gathering of a bountiful harvest, symbolic of a positive relationship between the Creator and His People; the beauty of our succah dwellings and of the *etrog* (a yellow citrus fruit), *lulav* (palm), myrtle and willow branches that are blessed on each day of the holiday (except Shabbat); the beginning of a blessed rainy season in the Land of Israel — all contribute to a national sense of euphoria.

Yet happiness is rarely commanded at will. Good actors can bring themselves to tears and laughter, but the tears are not of true grief and that laughter does not connote genuine happiness. True joy, such as the joy required of us on Succot, can only arise from deep inner resources. The Talmud observes that there are many routes to such happiness.

One of these is the joy inherent in resolving doubts. The Jewish People has always dealt with truth successfully. We find it more difficult to deal with fantasies, illusions and false prophecies. Thus, internalizing the truths of Judaism and of our Jewishness is one component of joy. The Talmudic rabbis also point out that knowledge of the past, especially the Jewish past, helps us achieve happiness. At the end of his life and career as leader of the Jewish People, Moses points out to his nation that by studying and knowing the past, Israel will always feel comforted, optimistic and of good cheer. We know this is true, even in the literal modern sense. Look at what the Jewish People has survived in the past century alone: the acts of hatred of various czars and kaisers; Hitler, Stalin, Nasser, Saddam Hussein. We have not only survived, in great measure we have flourished. Knowing and realizing this can open up the wellsprings of faith and happiness that lie deep within each and every one of us.

The strange thing about Succot is that it seemingly emphasizes our vulnerability. We reside for the seven days of the holiday in a temporary "booth," exposed to the elements, deprived of the comforts of our homes to which we are so accustomed. Torah law sees to it that this is the case: The very structure of a succah is impermanent and there is no roof over our heads. But it is this vulnerability that gives us satisfaction, for we realize while sitting in the succah that we are at all times dependent upon our Creator. Therefore, we are never alone in this dangerous world; we are under His protection. We realize that we are part of the great drama of Jewish history and that each of us has a leading and noble role to play in that drama; and that even though we are mortal and frightened, we are bound to something that is eternal and of priceless value. Such an understanding of life will radiate within us, resulting in the inner glow of joy and happiness that this great holiday is meant to bring.

Intermediate Days of Holidays:
41 Chol Hamoed

Both Passover and Succot are weeklong festivals. In the Land of Israel they are seven days in length, while in the Diaspora they are eight days in length. In Israel, the first and seventh days of Passover are full holidays, while in the Diaspora the first, second, seventh and eighth days are full holidays. On Succot, in Israel, the first day is a full holiday and in the Diaspora, the first two days are full holidays. The balance of the days of these holidays is called Chol Hamoed — the intermediate, less holy days of the holiday.

Torah mandated, this extremely sophisticated concept of days that are holidays, but not completely so, is a unique creation. Unlike the actual full holy days of the holidays, these intermediate days do not carry with them the entire gamut of restrictions on work. In fact, work that is necessary for comfort and/or to prevent monetary loss is permissible. However, the intermediate days are not to be treated as ordinary workdays. Unnecessary work, work that is easily postponed till after the holidays, law-suits and other contentious matters, etc. are not to be pursued during Chol Hamoed. Therefore, in Israel and in many parts of the Diaspora, Chol Hamoed is a vacation and leisure time. Stores and offices are closed and entire families participate in touring, visiting friends and relatives, attending concerts and participating in other forms of recreation.

Distinguishing it from a common weekday, on Chol Hamoed holiday clothing and finery are worn and festive meals are served. It is a joyous and sweet time of the year, especially for the children who are free of school and their routines for the week.

Chol Hamoed is a practical example of the Jewish ability to transform the everyday into the special and the mundane into holiness. We can all understand the concept of Sabbath and holidays and the fact that work is somehow inconsistent with the spirit and message of those days. But Chol Hamoed affords an opportunity to work and not work, celebrate and yet perform the tasks of everyday life. There is a ritual and rhythm to Chol Hamoed that governs this remarkable time. It is a time for family and friends, for study and reading, for relaxation and refreshment. But it is not summer vacation or midwinter break. It has holiness, ritual and legal parameters. And that it is what gives Chol Hamoed its special resonance and feeling in the Jewish world.

One of the customs of Chol Hamoed is to pay one's respects to great rabbis and scholars. In Israel, and in the Diaspora as well, the great rabbis, Chassidic leaders and heads of the yeshivot all hold open house during Chol Hamoed. There are Jews who travel from all corners of the world to visit their spiritual leaders and pay their homage to the Torah and its scholars. For their efforts, they come away with inspiration that lasts them all year.

In Jerusalem, there is a special "Blessing by the Kohanim" (descendants of the family of Aaron) ceremony conducted at the plaza of the Western Wall. Hundreds of priests gather there to bless the tens of thousands of Jews who gather at the Wall to receive their heavenly blessing on Chol Hamoed. It is a stirring event for all. Imagine thousands of people standing in perfect, reverent silence as the *tallit*-covered Kohanim lift their voices in hearty blessing.

During Chol Hamoed of Succot, there are parties held every night to celebrate the joyous "drawing of the water" — a ceremony that took place in the Temple in Jerusalem. The Talmud describes how this service was celebrated in Temple times with songs, dances, torches and bonfires, jugglers and performers. The "drawing of the water" from the Gichon Spring south of Jerusalem and its libation on the altar of the Temple symbolically marked the beginning of the rainy season in Israel and initiated the prayers for a bountiful rainfall during the winter months. The Talmud states that "sleep did not find our eyes" during these festive Chol Hamoed nights. That still is pretty much the case for the young today during Chol Hamoed celebrations, for though the Temple and its altar are not now present, the celebrations of Chol Hamoed Succot have survived and prospered. Throughout Jerusalem's many neighborhoods, the parties and celebrations take place deep into the night. All of Jerusalem seems to be singing for a solid week.

Outside of Israel, similar Chol Hamoed celebrations are held in many Jewish communities. The mood is light; hearts are merry as Jews feel a festive connection with Jews worldwide who are also enjoying the unique pleasure of this special time.

Shmini Atzeret
and Simchat Torah

s the Succot festival ends, the special holidays of Shmini Atzeret and Simchat Torah begin. In reality, Shmini Atzeret is a holiday unto itself, a day added to Succot when Jews are bidden to enjoy yet one more day of closeness to God, without fanfare or ritual. When the Jews went into exile from their homeland of the Land of Israel, they also adopted the custom of keeping a second day of the holidays as per the Talmud. Thus, Shmini Atzeret, regarded practically as the eighth day of Succot, so to speak, also had a second day added to it outside of Israel. As Shmini Atzeret has no special *mitzvot* (commandments) connected to it except that of rejoicing, the "second day" of Shmini Atzeret is Simchat Torah, a day of great rejoicing with the Torah. In present-day Israel, where only one day of the holiday is observed, Shmini Atzeret and Simchat Torah are celebrated simultaneously on the same day.

Whereas on Shavuot we commemorate the anniversary of the granting of Torah to the Jewish nation at Mount

Sinai, on Simchat Torah we simply rejoice in the fact that we possess the holy Torah. Simchat Torah is different from all other holidays in the Jewish calendar year in that it is not based on Biblical, Talmudic or rabbinic literature. It is a holiday that emanated from within the Jewish People to express its love and appreciation for Torah. The celebration on Simchat Torah, like all Jewish events that have survived the test of time and changing societal circumstances, follows a ritual, a halachic standard.

Most of the customs that form the basis of our present day Simchat Torah celebration arose between the thirteenth and sixteenth centuries in Central Europe and then spread throughout the remainder of the Jewish world. The focus of Simchat Torah is the fact that the public Torah readings of every Sabbath throughout the year come to their conclusion on Simchat Torah. The ancient custom of Babylonian Jewry to complete the reading of the Torah every year was adopted by world Jewry in the fifth century.

The final portion of the Torah is read many times over on Simchat Torah in order to accommodate the custom of calling every adult male to the Torah for an *aliyah*. The final person called to complete the Torah reading is called the *Chattan Torah* — the bridegroom of the Torah. A *tallit* is spread over the *Chattan* and the Torah and serves as a *chupah*, a wedding canopy, symbolizing the eternal love bond between the Torah and the People of Israel.

The cycle of the reading of the Torah is now commenced immediately and another *Chattan, Chattan Bereshit,* is called to the Torah and the first section of the Torah, *Bereshit*/Genesis, is now read aloud, again under the canopy of the *tallit*. The Torah reading is preceded by seven *hakafot* — circling processions carrying all of the Torahs from the ark of the synagogue. These processions are accompanied by songs, dancing (and unofficially, liquid refreshment) and a great spirit of merriment and joy.

A special *aliyah* to the Torah that includes all of the children present, even infants, takes place. It is deemed a particular honor for the adult who leads the children in the blessings over the Torah as this *aliyah*, called *Kol Hanaarim*, signifies the continuity of Torah study and observance among the Jewish People over all of its generations. It is the guarantee of our future. For as long as there is Torah in Israel and the love of that Torah is transmitted to our children, we will survive and flourish. Simchat Torah is the day of connection to Torah; it is therefore a wonderful opportunity to help our children recognize the value of Torah and count themselves among the Jewish People.

43 **Chanukah**

The holiday of Chanukah is rabbinic in origin (as is Purim), rather than written in the Torah, and commemorates the successful uprising of the Jewish people in approximately 165 BCE against the rule of the Syrian Greeks over the Land of Israel and the Temple in Jerusalem. The Greeks had de facto control of the Land of Israel from the time of Alexander the Great, 150 years earlier. However, for a long period of time, they did not interfere with the internal and religious life of the Jewish people and the Jews were willing to tolerate the nominal Greek control of the country.

Gradually, however, the influence of Greek culture and paganism prompted a segment of the Jewish people to become assimilated and Hellenized; this meant abandoning Jewish custom and practice and becoming a willing agent for further Greek penetration into Jewish society. As has sadly often happened in Jewish history, these Hellenized Jews came to despise their more loyal and observant brethren and enlisted the aid of the Greek authorities to coerce their fellow Jews into becoming "more relevant" to modern Greek society. The Greek authorities, at the behest and cooperation of the Hellenists, banned circumcision, forced Jews to eat the flesh of swine, erected a statue of Zeus in the Temple in Jerusalem and coerced Jewish women to submit to Greek officers before being allowed to marry.

These, and other outrages, caused the Jews to finally take up arms and fight a war to expel the Greeks from the country, to destroy the Hellenists and to rededicate the Temple in Jerusalem to the service of the God of Israel. This rebellion was led by a family of Kohanim (priests of Israel) known as both Hasmoneans and Maccabees. The elder of the family, Mattityahu, and four of his sons, Yochanan, Yehudah ("Judah Maccabee"), Yonatan and Elazar, all died during the war. The sole surviving son, Shimon, saw the victory over the Greeks and became the High Priest and leader of the Jewish people, establishing a ruling Hasmonean dynasty that lasted for 103 years.

After cleansing the Temple of its Greek idols, the Jews lit the great golden Menorah — the seven-branched candelabrum. The small jar of sacred oil that supplied the fuel for the light of the Menorah contained oil sufficient for one day's supply. However, miraculously, the fuel lasted for eight days, long enough for new pure olive oil for the Temple to be manufactured. In honor of this miracle and in commemoration of the victory of the Hasmoneans over the Greeks and the Jewish Hellenists, the rabbis instituted the eight-day holiday of Chanukah.

The special eight-branched Chanukah candelabra are lit in our homes every night of the holiday, starting with only one candle or oil light. Each night another light is added, until on the eighth night of Chanukah all eight of the candles or oil lights are lit and the house is filled with their light, warmth and memory. An extra candle — a *shamash* (servant) — is lit every night as well. It is used to light the other lights and it is placed higher or on the side of the regular candles or oil lights. The candelabrum is commonly called a menorah, an allusion to the seven-branched Menorah that stood in the Temple. A more accurate appellation for it is *Chanukiah*, i.e. a candelabrum specifically designed to publicize the miracles of Chanukah. As its purpose is to enlighten the world about the lessons of Chanukah and reinforce faith, it is prominently placed in a window or doorway.

Because of the miracle of the olive oil it is customary to eat foods that are fried in oil. Though perhaps not recommended dietetically, Jews traditionally eat Chanukah doughnuts and potato latkes (pancakes), all of which are fried in oil. Bismarck pastries (doughnuts with cream filling, called *sufganiot* in Israel) are also popular. The children are given *Chanukah gelt* (money) in honor of the festive holiday; and the rabbis wisely looked away at the Jewish custom of playing cards or *dreidel* (a specially marked top) for money on the holiday of Chanukah. Even these latter customs of gambling are memory aids to the original Chanukah, for when the Hasmoneans gathered to plan their attacks against the Greeks, they did so under the cover that a gambling event or gaming night was taking place. The custom of giving toys and other gifts is relatively recent, perhaps in imitation of the gift-giving season of Christian society.

Chanukah has become one of the most popular and beloved weeks in the Jewish calendar. It renews our faith in the eternity of the Torah and the Jewish people; it promises our eventual victory over assimilation; and it endorses our firm stand against tyranny, discrimination and violent subjugation. The small flames of our *Chanukiah* light our life not only for one week, but for all time as well.

44 The Hasmoneans

The Hasmonean family ruled the Jewish state in the Land of Israel for 103 years after the liberation of Jerusalem from the Syrian Greeks and their Hellenized Jewish allies in 165 BCE. The Hasmoneans were Kohanim, descendants of Aaron. After their triumph, Shimon, the leader of the family and the last surviving son of Mattityahu, assumed the mantle of *Kohen Gadol*, the High Priest in the Temple. Shimon refused to proclaim himself officially as king, since the monarchy, by tradition, belonged to the tribe of Judah, the descendants of the House of David. However, he did install himself as the temporal ruler over the Jews and for all practical purposes served as the king. Shimon was an extremely pious, fair and wise person and was able to successfully serve as High Priest and "king" simultaneously.

Nevertheless, the rabbinic leadership of the time disapproved of this political/spiritual arrangement of joint power in one person. Ever mindful of how assuredly and insidiously power corrupts, the rabbis favored a diffusion of power among many people instead of a concentration of power in one person, or even in an oligarchy. But since Shimon was of unassailable character and gifted performance, this objection was muted during his lifetime. The rabbis were also very troubled by the Hasmonean policy of "convincing" the Idumean tribe living in the south of Israel to convert to Judaism. These Idumeans were excellent soldiers and eventually came to make up the private guard of the Hasmonean kings. Judaism is not a proselytizing faith and therefore converts to Judaism were accepted only if the sincerity of the convert was apparent. Coerced conversions, such as in the case with the Idumeans, were regarded as contrary to the letter and spirit of Torah law. Thus was laid the foundation of the ongoing struggle of the rabbis — called the *Perushim* — against the rule of the later Hasmonean kings.

The descendants of Shimon were not his equals in wisdom, character and piety. Civil wars over dynastic succession, abuse of both of the high offices combined in one person, a strategic error of monumental proportion of inviting Rome into Israel to "protect" the Jews from the Greeks, and the fact that the later Hasmonean kings left the fold of Jewish tradition and became Sadducees (*Tzadokim*) — all combined to sour the rabbis and the majority of Jews in Israel on the Hasmoneans and their rule. At the time of Alexander Janneus, the strongest and most militaristic of the Hasmonean kings, an actual civil war between the *Perushim* and the king's forces took place. Many thousands of Jews were slain by other Jews in what was one of the saddest chapters of Jewish history.

The Hasmonean dynasty, begun by Mattityahu and Shimon in the blaze of the miraculous lights of Chanukah, ended ignominiously with the accession of Antipater the Idumean and later his son, Herod, to the leadership of the government. These Idumeans now were appointees and puppets of Rome and the Jewish people groaned under their rapacious and murderous rule. Eventually, Herod killed the last surviving member of the Hasmonean family. The rabbis of the Talmud ruefully commented that "anyone who today claims to be of the house of the Hasmoneans is in fact a descendant of Herod and is thus a 'slave' in pedigree!"

The Jewish people prefer to remember the beginnings of the Hasmoneans and not their self-inflicted sad and disappointing end. They remain in the Jewish mind as the great heroes of the Chanukah story, as holy High Priests, as champions of the Jewish spirit and the will to remain loyal Jews, no matter what the odds and difficulties. Yet we also would do well to view their legacy as a demonstration of how the human traits of greed, lust for power and treachery are given rein when allegiance to the Torah and its values are lost.

45 The Tenth of Tevet

This fast day is one of the four fast days that commemorate dark times in Jewish history. The other three are:

- [ ] the Ninth of Av, the day of the destruction of both Temples in Jerusalem;
- [ ] the Seventeenth of Tamuz, the day the defensive wall of Jerusalem was breached by Titus and the Roman legions in 70 CE;
- [ ] the third of Tishrei, known as the Fast of Gedaliah, the day that marks the assassination of the Babylonian-appointed Jewish governor of Judah, Gedaliah ben Achikam. (He was actually killed on Rosh Hashanah, but the fast day was advanced to the day after Rosh Hashanah because of the holiday.)

The Tenth of Tevet marks the onset of the siege of Jerusalem by Nebuchadnezzar, the king of Babylonia, and the beginning of the battle that ultimately destroyed

Jerusalem and the Temple of Solomon, sending the Jews into the seventy-year Babylonian Exile. The date of the Tenth of Tevet is recorded for us by the prophet Ezekiel, who himself was already in Babylonia as part of the first group of Jews exiled there by Nebuchadnezzar, eleven years earlier than the actual destruction of the Temple in Jerusalem. The Tenth of Tevet is viewed as such a severe and important fast day that it is observed even if it falls on a Friday (before Shabbat), while our other fast days are arranged by calendar adjustments as to never fall on a Friday.

However, there are other commemorative days that fall immediately before the Tenth of Tevet and their memory has been silently incorporated in the fast day of the Tenth of Tevet. On the eighth of Tevet, King Ptolemy of Egypt forced seventy Jewish scholars to gather and translate the Hebrew Bible into Greek. Even though the Talmud relates to us that this project was blessed with a miracle — the seventy scholars were all placed in separate cubicles and yet they all came up with the same translation — the general view of the Jews of the time towards this project was decidedly negative. The Talmud records that when this translation became public, "darkness descended on the world." This translation — the Septuagint — eventually became the basis for the Old Testament section of the Christian Bible a few centuries later. The Greek translation of the Bible also aided the agenda of the Hellenist Jews to bring Greek culture into Jewish life, attempting to reform Judaism in the image of Greek values and lifestyle. The "koshering" of the Greek language by its use in translating the Hebrew Bible had wide ramifications in Jewish society and undermined Jewish efforts to combat the allure of Greece in Israel at that time.

The ninth day of Tevet is held to be the day of the death of Ezra the Scribe. This great Jew is comparable to Moses in the eyes of the Talmud. "If the Torah had not been granted through Moses, it could have been granted to Israel through Ezra." Ezra led the return of the Jews to Jerusalem from their Babylonian exile. It was under his direction and inspiration, with the help of Nechemiah, that the Second Temple was built, albeit originally on a much more modest scale and style than the grandeur of King Solomon's Temple. Ezra also renewed the covenant of Moses between Israel and God; staunched the flow of intermarriage that afflicted the Jews returning to Jerusalem; strengthened public and private Sabbath observance and created the necessary schools and intellectual tools for the furtherance of the knowledge and development of the Oral Law of Sinai within the Jewish People. A man of incorruptible character, great compassion, deep vision, erudition and inspirational charisma, Ezra the Scribe is responsible for the survival of Judaism and the Jews till this very day. It is no wonder, therefore, that Jews marked the day of his death as a sad day on the Jewish calendar. Since fasting on the eighth, ninth and tenth days of Tevet consecutively would be unreasonable, the events of the eighth and ninth were subsumed into the fast day of the Tenth of Tevet.

46 The Fast of Esther

The two major fast days in the Jewish calendar year are Yom Kippur and the Ninth of Av, the day of the destruction of the First and Second Temples. However, there are other lesser fast days observed. One of these occurs on the day before Purim: It is called the Fast of Esther. In the Book of Esther, which is read publicly in the synagogue services on Purim, we are told that Esther and the entire Jewish population of Shushan (capital of ancient Persia) fasted for three days as a sign of repentance. It was a desperate attempt to access Divine intervention to save them from the Vizier Haman's evil decree of genocide. This period of fasting took place immediately after the announcement of Haman's decree. According to Jewish tradition, Haman's decree coincided with the beginning of the holiday of Passover. The Jews therefore fasted on Passover in that time of dire trouble and danger. Because fasting on holidays is inappropriate in Jewish law and custom, the commemoration of those fast days in ancient Shushan was moved to the thirteenth day of Adar, the day that precedes Purim for most of the Jewish world. It was also shortened to a one-day fast. It is called the Fast of Esther, since she was the one who first ordained it as a day of prayer and penance, and for other deeper reasons, explained below.

The symbolism of the fast day is obvious. The Jewish People, small in numbers and different always in its faith, beliefs and lifestyle from the dominant cultures and societies around them, has been easily victimized in its long history. Jews always represent the ultimate "other" in human civilization. In a world where the "other" is not always easily tolerated, there was and still is inherent danger in being the "other." Haman's scapegoating of the Jews for his own power hungry motives is the classic Biblical example of that danger. The Fast of Esther therefore serves as a constant reminder to Jews of the potential difficulties of our situation vis-à-vis the cultures and governments of the world. It clearly emphasizes the Jewish belief that Divine intervention has spared the Jewish people from extinction and that despite all of the Hamans of history, Israel has survived and even prospered.

The Fast of Esther therefore proclaims our loyalty and gratitude to God for so preserving us, and it allows us to have a sense of introspection, spirituality and historical perspective that make the immediately forthcoming Purim celebration meaningful and truly joyous. Because of its immediate proximity to the celebrations of Purim, the Fast of Esther is the least somber in tone of the fast days. The other fast days all deal with the loss of Jerusalem and the Land of Israel and, so to speak, have not achieved a completely happy ending to the Jewish story as of yet. However, even while fasting on the Fast Day of Esther, we are aware of the triumph of Esther and Mordechai over Haman and our mood of solemnity and somberness is somewhat mitigated by our knowing the happy ending to Esther's story.

Let us consider Queen Esther, the great Jewish heroine of the story of Purim. She risked everything — position, wealth, even life itself — to plead the cause of her people and to upset Haman's nefarious plans. The Jewish nation has kept her noble memory alive. Over thousands of years, Jewish girls have been given her name (Hadassah in its Hebrew form, and Esther in its Persian form). Her heroism and loyalty to her people have made her a symbol of Jewish life and continuity. It is not surprising therefore that the rabbis and People of Israel have chosen to name this fast day of commemoration and spiritual preparation in her honor.

The Fast of Esther, then, reminds us not only of troubles and persecution, but of heroic figures in the Jewish world as well. All of Jewish history indicates that God responds to such noble figures and to individual and collective Jewish heroism. Esther lives on in our collective memory as the symbol of deliverance from evil and of Godly grace upon the People of Israel.

47 **Purim**

The holiday of Purim commemorates the miraculous deliverance of the Jewish People from the genocidal decree of Haman, the Vizier of Persia, in the fourth century BCE. Using the classic tactics of anti-Semites then and ever since, Haman scapegoats the Jews as being the cause of all the problems that the Emperor Achashverus encounters in governing his sprawling, polyglot, 127-nation empire. Haman corrupts the Emperor by promising him vast riches from the booty of the annihilated Jews. Haman's plans, however, are thwarted by the intervention of God through the actions of Queen Esther and her uncle, Mordechai. Haman ends up swinging from the 100-foot tall gallows that he had constructed for the execution of Mordechai; his evil decree is countermanded. The Jews of the empire rise in self-defense, and the intended day of doom becomes a day of Jewish rejoicing and thankfulness. This entire series of events was recorded by Esther and Mordechai, in what is known today as the Megillah, or the Book of Esther. The rabbis of the time, following the request of Esther, proclaimed the fourteenth and fifteenth days of the Hebrew month of Adar (on which the Jews were saved from extermination), as eternal days of celebration and joy on the Jewish calendar, and so have they remained till this very day.

The precise day of Purim varies according to where Jewish communities are located. The vast majority of Jews the world over commemorate the day on the fourteenth of Adar. However, Jews who live in communities that were once walled cities, such as the then capitol city of the Persian Empire itself, Shushan, celebrate Purim on the fifteenth of Adar, as per the instructions recorded in the Book of Esther itself. Thus, Jerusalem, Tiberias, Damascus and other ancient communities celebrate Purim on the fifteenth day of Adar.

The mode of Purim celebrations revolves around four practices that are part of the halachic ritual of the day. The first of these is the public reading of the Book of Esther in the synagogue on the night of Purim and again in the morning. A custom hallowed by the ages and generations of mischievous Jewish children to boo, hiss and make derogatory sounds every time the name of Haman is mentioned during the reading of the Megillah, is universal. The contest between the children and the public reader, in his attempt to subdue the length and intensity of the clamor, is in itself one of the treasured experiences of Purim. Traditionally, the children win this battle.

Other halachically-mandated events are centered on acts of friendship, kindness to others, giving charity to the poor and family bonding. Gifts of food are exchanged between friends, alms are given generously to all who ask for them and a festive family meal is held in the late afternoon of Purim. Because of the fact that the miracle of Purim was a "hidden" one, i.e. it was brought about through seemingly natural political events and coincidences, Jews dress in costumes, masks and other "disguises" on Purim.

In a remarkable departure from Jewish norms, the Talmud also allows one to become inebriated on Purim, and the consuming of liquor and wine is part of the celebration of the day. Purim plays, masquerades, costumes, parades and other forms of musical and dramatic entertainment also are customary. Dancing, singing and merriment are the general rule. In short, Purim is a day of pure joy.

The Talmud declares that even when all of the other holidays of the Jewish year will be obviated by the arrival of the Messianic Era, Purim will continue to be commemorated. Purim is the testimony to Jewish survival, to the triumph of good over evil, to God's intervention in human events to preserve His Holy Name and His People. So "Happy Purim" is more than a greeting. It is a statement of faith and hope and optimism in the coming of a better world.

Passover and
48 The Spring Calendar

The holiday of Passover is the foundation stone of the Jewish calendar. In the Torah we read: "This month (Nissan) is unto you the first of all months of the year." Thus, even though the count of the Jewish year changes in the fall with Rosh Hashanah in the month of Tishrei, the month that determines the calendar of the year itself is Nissan. If you think that this in itself is not complicated enough, brace yourself and read on. The Jewish calendar is basically a lunar calendar. As such, the Jewish year contains only 354 days (six months that are 30 days long and six months that are 29 days long). As we all know, the solar year, which is the Western, Christian calendar year, is 365 days long. Thus, there is a differential of 11 days between the solar calendar and the shorter lunar year. Are you with me so far?

In the event that there would be no built-in adjustments made in the Jewish calendar, the holiday of Passover would slip back one solar month every three years. Thus in 2001 it was in April, but in 2004 it would be in March and in 2007 in February and in 2010 in January, in the dead of winter in the Northern Hemisphere! The Torah, however, forbids this from happening for it tells us, "Today you leave Egypt in the month of spring." The Jewish laws derived from Sinai therefore cautioned us to always make certain that Passover, in the month of Nissan, should fall in the spring in the Northern Hemisphere. The task of setting the yearly Jewish calendar devolved upon the Sanhedrin, and their main guiding point was that the lunar calendar of Israel had to be reconciled with the solar calendar so that Passover would always be a spring holiday.

The primary mechanism for this reconciliation was the addition of a thirteenth lunar month to the lunar year every so often. In its discussion of the calendar in Tractates *Rosh Hashanah* and *Sanhedrin*, the Talmud describes some of the factors — weather, social conditions, crops in the field — that went into this judicial discussion and decree. The Sanhedrin operated as the controller of the calendar for a thousand years, from the time of Moses until the fifth century of the Common Era, when under Roman and Christian pressure it was forced to abandon the Land of Israel and eventually disband. However, as a last act of service to the Jewish people, the Sanhedrin developed the permanent Jewish calendar that serves the Jews even today.

The basic premise of the permanent Jewish calendar is that the sun and the moon operate relative to each other in nineteen-year cycles. Thus by having seven thirteen-month lunar years — "leap years" — within that nineteen year solar-lunar cycle, the two calendar year cycles would be generally reconciled. "Second Adar" is the additional month added before Nissan and Passover. In order to further fine-tune this reconciliation, two "swing" months were allowed in the Jewish calendar — MarCheshvan and Kislev — each of which could be either twenty-nine or thirty days long, depending on the reconciliation requirements of any given year. I hope that you are still with me, because there is at least one more consideration that must be taken into account.

This consideration is that Yom Kippur cannot fall on a Friday or a Sunday. This is because burials would then have to be delayed for two days — the Sabbath and Yom Kippur — and such delays, in general principle, are contrary to Jewish law and custom. Thus, all of the days upon which any of the Jewish holidays of the year may fall are dependent upon the placement of Yom Kippur on a day other than Sunday or Friday.

So the important Jewish calendar rules to remember are that Passover must always fall in the Northern Hemisphere in the spring and that Yom Kippur will never fall on a Friday or Sunday. This information should suffice to impress your neighbors with your Jewish erudition!

49 Selling the Chametz

O ne of the institutions of traditional life as far as Passover preparations are concerned is the "selling of the *chametz*." The Torah commands Jews not only not to eat *chametz* during the week of Passover, but also not to possess *chametz* during that time. For many Jews, both in ancient and modern times, that rule is simply met by removing all *chametz* from one's home and property and disposing of it by destroying it or giving it away to non-Jews. For many centuries, most Jews were able to deal with their *chametz* in this simple manner. There was no uniform, institutionalized method in Jewish life to make certain that *chametz* was not owned by Jews on the holiday.

This situation began to change in the late Middle Ages. The catalyst for this change was the fact that Jews were increasingly involved in the production and sale of liquor in Europe. Almost all liquor was made from a fermented grain base and thus was *chametz*. Jews who owned distilleries, warehouses or taverns full of barrels and bottles of liquor were faced with a crisis when Passover came, since they could not possess that liquor during the holiday. To destroy it or give it away would result in tremendous financial loss. To further compound the dilemma that they faced, there is a rabbinic prohibition against deriving any benefit from *chametz* that was owned by a Jew during Passover, even after Passover ends. To meet the exigencies of the situation, the formal sale of *chametz* to a non-Jew for the Passover time period was initiated by rabbis sensitive to their plight.

This sale had to accomplish two things: Firstly it had to be legal and binding, that in truth the non-Jew was the actual owner of the *chametz* during Passover. Secondly, the sale had to be so arranged that the Jew would be able to repurchase the *chametz* from the non-Jew after the holiday for a nominal amount. If this second aim was not achieved, then the whole purpose of the sale would be defeated, for the Jew would not be able to remain in business if he had to pay a huge sum for the return of the merchandise. The rabbis therefore invested a great deal of ingenuity and creativity in structuring the sale so it would be truly legal, and yet the Jew would be protected as far as his rights of repurchase after Passover was concerned.

The drive for full legality of this very technical sale was so strong that a question arose in the nineteenth century in the Austro-Hungarian Empire. There, the government had instituted a law that tax stamps had to be affixed to all contracts of sale. The documents of sale that the rabbis used for selling *chametz* to non-Jews never contained such tax stamps and thus some in the Jewish community questioned the legality of the sale. The rabbis of Austria-Hungary appealed to the emperor to issue a special waiver of the necessity for tax stamps on the sale of *chametz*. The emperor did, in fact, issue that waiver, based on the understanding that the sale was necessary in order to fulfill a Jewish religious obligation. The emperor's reasoning in itself was disturbing, since it somehow implied that this was a "religious sale" and not a commercial transaction. Ultimately, however, the rabbis deemed the sale sufficiently legal to satisfy the Jewish legal requirement that the *chametz* was not possessed by Jews over the Passover holiday.

The rabbi of the community usually was given a fee for representing the entire Jewish community in arranging for the sale of the *chametz* to a trustworthy non-Jew. It also became a source of income, sometimes significant, to the trustworthy non-Jews who annually bought the *chametz* from the Jewish community. Many times, the right to buy the Jewish *chametz* passed down by inheritance from father to son. Thus, it was not only the Jews who looked forward to the coming of Passover and the celebration of Jewish freedom.

Today, as in years past, observant Jews contact their rabbi to represent them in this legally complex sale of their household *chametz,* as well as that used in business. The rabbi explains that the *chametz* may remain in the Jew's home, as long as it is accessible to the non-Jew should he want to take possession of it. After Passover, the rabbi informs his congregation at what time the *chametz* has been repurchased in their behalf. Since buying *chametz* that was owned by a Jew during Passover is forbidden, observant Jews are careful where they purchase their breads, cereals, liquor etc. for several weeks after the holiday.

50 Matzoh Shmurah

n the Torah it is written: "And you shall guard the matzot." Guard them from what? And how shall they be guarded? The written words of the Torah are always very cryptic, the Torah itself relying upon the accompanying Oral Law to explain and exposit its meaning in practical terms and rules of behavior. The matzot of Passover are to be "guarded" from the possibility of their becoming *chametz* — leavened. To accomplish this guarding, Passover matzoh must be thoroughly baked within eighteen minutes of the water touching the flour at the beginning of the kneading process. As a further safeguard, the matzot that are used at the Seder for the *mitzvah* of eating matzoh must be *matzoh shmurah* — literally, guarded matzot. The "guarding" consists of special rabbinic supervision to ensure that no water touched the flour even before the actual process of the kneading of the dough.

There are two leading opinions in Jewish law as to when this period of guarding must begin. The more lenient opinion, which is supported in theory by most of the rabbinic commentators, states that the "guarding" begins with the milling of the grain into flour. Wheat, barley, rye, spelt and oats are the acceptable grains for matzoh. From the milling moment onwards, the flour is guarded against any contamination of water or dampness that could cause a question of leavening — *chametz* — to rise. The more conservative opinion, which in practice governs throughout the Jewish world today, is that the guarding commences at the moment of the harvesting of the grain. As long as the grain is yet attached to the earth, no matter how much water may fall on it, there can be no question of *chametz*. Once the grain is cut away from its base in the earth, the problem of dampness, water and *chametz* commences. Thus *matzoh shmurah* today is made from grain that was "guarded" from the moment it was cut and then throughout the entire milling and baking process, in order to make certain that no possibility of *chametz* could arise.

There are certain fields of grain in the United States and Israel that are contracted specially to produce grain for *matzoh shmurah*. After the grain has ripened fully in the early fall, and dry weather has prevailed for a number of days, it stands ready to be cut. Rabbinic representatives of the matzoh baking companies will then gather at the farm to supervise the harvesting and packaging of the grain that will then be sent directly to the miller, where other rabbinic representatives will supervise the transformation of the raw grain into flour for matzoh baking. After the grain is milled, it is packed into 100 pound sacks, and special rabbinic marks of designation are placed on and within the sacks certifying that this flour may be used for the baking of *matzoh shmurah*. The sacks of flour are then stacked high on pallets to keep them off the floor in storerooms, with circulating fans operating to prevent any possibility of dampness affecting the flour. Because of these many levels of careful supervision, *matzoh shmurah* usually sells for a higher price than the other kosher for Passover matzot.

Many people use hand-baked *shmurah matzot* for the Seder as a remembrance of the matzoh eaten by our ancestors on that first Passover night in Egypt. Hand-baked *matzoh shmurah* is usually more expensive than its machine-baked counterpart. All of the matzoh bakeries produce *matzoh shmurah* and there are Jews who eat only *matzoh shmurah* during the entire holiday of Passover. I don't know why, and I am certain that it is purely psychological, but *matzoh shmurah* always tasted different — even better — to me than the regular Passover matzot. And I'm told that I'm not alone in this opinion.

51 "Machine" Matzoh

No holiday has the volume of published halachic (Jewish legal) literature concerning it that Passover has. The questions under discussion reflect Jewish life throughout the centuries and in all of the countries and circumstances of the long Jewish exile.

In the mid-1850's, as the Industrial Revolution gained momentum in Central and Eastern Europe, an ingenious inventor in the Austro-Hungarian Empire created a machine to bake matzot. Until that time, matzot were always baked by hand. They were usually round in form and no two matzot were exactly the same in size, color or consistency. Customarily, each family baked its own matzot individually, though by the early part of the eighteenth century there were many commercial matzoh bakeries throughout the Jewish world. The matzoh baking in those bakeries was done by hand and almost all of the workers were women, usually widows who were able to live (survive would be a better word) the rest of the year on the money they earned in the months of matzoh baking.

The work was physically very demanding and tension laden, since the matzoh had to be completely baked within eighteen minutes of the time that water touched the flour at the beginning of the kneading process. The rabbinic literature of the ages is replete with warnings to owners of matzoh bakeries not to exploit or verbally abuse the workers, especially the widows, during this tension-filled time.

The invention of the matzoh-baking machine raised a furor in the rabbinic world. Great rabbis permitted the use of the matzoh-baking machine, and in fact preferred its products to the hand-baked matzot. The machine did not get tired at four in the afternoon, its products were uniform and well baked, and the machine suffered naught from any remarks addressed to it. It also allowed for lower prices for matzoh and produced far greater amounts of the food to be distributed for the Passover holiday. However, there was also rabbinic opposition to the new matzoh-baking machine. This disagreement reached bitter proportions in the first decades of its use.

There were two main objections to the machine. One was the social and economic dislocation that new technology always creates to individuals trapped in the old way of doing things. The rabbis who opposed the matzoh-baking machine came to the defense of the poor women who were rendered useless by the introduction of the new machinery. Such social concerns are an integral part of all rabbinic literature throughout the ages, no matter what the actual issue involved. The second objection dealt with the fact that small bits of dough could remain in the machine for longer than eighteen minutes and thus became the forbidden *chametz*. Potentially, these bits of clogged matter could find their way into the matzoh itself, rendering it unfit for Passover use.

Most of the Chassidic communities in Eastern Europe chose not to use the machine-made matzot on Passover. However, the machine matzoh gained popularity among the rest of Jewish society, especially in the United States and Israel. Technological improvements in the matzoh-baking machines have occurred over the century and a half since its introduction, so the objections to the original machines are no longer valid. Nevertheless, today there are many Jewish families that use hand-baked matzot, especially for the Seder itself.

It is obvious that our ancestors did not use machine-baked matzoh when they left Egypt. Thus the tradition of eating hand-baked matzot has its place, even in our technologically advanced world, as a symbolic reminder of the Exodus from Egyptian bondage.

Legumes on Passover: 52 Kitnayot

There is perhaps no area of Jewish law where the Jewish People have taken upon themselves more stringencies than regarding the prohibition of possessing or eating *chametz* (leavened foods) on Passover. Jews have always been very diligent in removing any possibility of error in this regard. Many customs that accumulated over the centuries in different locales have become part of our regular Passover observance. Because of these regional differences, not all Jewish communities share the same customs. The Ashkenazic and Sephardic communities differ on the eating or avoidance of *kitnayot*, loosely defined as foods derived from legumes.

Such foods as peas, beans, soy, corn/maize (which was unknown in Europe until the seventeenth century), mustard seed and rice are included in the Ashkenazic ban on *kitnayot*. This custom developed among Ashkenazic Jewry in the Middle Ages in Central and Eastern Europe, though the origins of the custom date back to pre-medieval times in the Balkans and Asia Minor. The custom developed for two distinct reasons: One was that kernels of wheat or barley were sometimes mixed inadvertently with rice, mustard seed, etc. and these kernels of wheat could potentially turn into *chametz* on Passover if they were exposed to water. Because of this possibility, many Sephardic communities that never adopted the custom of banning other forms of *kitnayot* on Passover nevertheless abstained from eating rice on Passover. Rabbi Yom Tov ben Avraham ibn Ashbili (Ritva), one of the great Sephardic Torah scholars of fourteenth century Spain, records that once wheat kernels were found to be mixed together with the rice in containers sold allegedly as pure rice, and therefore the Sephardim in northern Spain refused to eat rice on Passover, while continuing to eat beans, peas and other forms of *kitnayot*. However, most Sephardim then and now continued to eat rice on Passover, as they do with all of the other forms of *kitnayot*.

The second reason that Ashkenazim banned the eating of *kitnayot* on Passover was because of the fact that "bread" was made from the flour of these various foods. This was because of economic, social or agricultural reasons. As such, there was fear that if one type of "bread" were allowed, *kitnayot* bread, real grain bread would also find its way to the Jewish table on Passover. Because of this concern, the use of *kitnayot* in any form was forbidden.

The question of what constitutes *kitnayot* occupies a significant place in rabbinic literature. Liquids and oils produced from *kitnayot* is also a source of discussion in rabbinic circles. Even today, there are different customs regarding these oils and syrups. In general, today they are not used, which is why soft drinks produced for Passover are sweetened with sugar and not with the corn syrup that is used the rest of the year.

In Israel, where the majority of the population is of Sephardic origin, many of the manufactured foods for Passover contain *kitnayot* or their oils. Therefore, Ashkenazim in Israel must exert great care in purchasing any foods for Passover. They must first ascertain that no *kitnayot* or *kitnayot* derivative is present in foods marked "Kosher for Passover." Though this can be a chore, it also lends a sense of adventure to the pre-Passover shopping in Israel. In any event, customs and stringencies have preserved the nation of Israel over the millennia, and the prohibition of *kitnayot* is a good example of this Jewish historical rule.

53 The Seder

The most meaningful family meal in Jewish life takes place every year on the first night of Passover. This meal — the Seder — relives and retells the story of the Jewish exodus from Egyptian bondage. Jewish tradition ascribes the year 1312 BCE as the year of "the Exodus." One of the reasons that families gather for this meal, often including several generations, is actually rooted in Jewish law. A primary *mitzvah* of Passover is the telling of the Passover story and specifically passing it on to the next generation. Since 1313 BCE, Jewish families have gathered their families every Passover to teach their children of the wondrous miracles of our redemption from Egypt — and we do so to this day.

The word *Seder* in Hebrew means "order" or "progression." The Seder meal is divided into a number of sections, each having bearing and symbolism regarding the history that is being reenacted that night. The centerpiece of the Seder meal is the participation of all gathered round the table in the festivities and the recitation of the Haggadah — the telling of the story of the redemption of the Jewish People from Egyptian bondage. Most Haggadot include instructions on how to conduct each ritual.

Special roles are assigned to the young children in the family in order to pique their interest and guarantee their participation in the Seder. The children (or at least the youngest child present) ask the "Four Questions" as to why the night of Passover differs from all other nights. Gifts and rewards are traditionally given to the children who ask the "Four Questions."

Three matzot are stacked on the table before the leader of the Seder. The middle matzoh is broken into two pieces and the larger piece is then hidden away as the *afikoman*. This *afikoman* is representative of the Paschal lamb that was eaten at the Seder meal in Jerusalem during Temple times. The young people at the Seder attempt to "steal" the *afikoman* and hold it for ransom before returning it at the conclusion of the meal. This exercise in legitimate thievery keeps the children up and about for the entire time of the meal. Clever, eh?

During the Seder, four cups of wine (or at least, grape juice) are consumed. These represent the four forms of physical and spiritual redemption that comprised the Exodus. A fifth cup of wine is poured in honor of the Prophet Elijah, who symbolically visits all Jewish homes on the Seder night. The door is opened for him and a prayer of welcome and of the hoped-for destruction of evil in the world is recited. No one drinks from Elijah's cup, though the children carefully look at the contents of the cup after the door is closed to check if perhaps Elijah took a sip.

The main rituals of the Seder consist of:

☐ eating the matzoh
☐ the recitation of the Haggadah (i.e. telling the story)
☐ eating bitter herbs which recall our bondage (the bitter herbs are dipped into charoset (a mixture of apples, wine, nuts, cinnamon and ginger) to remind us of the lime pits of Egypt in which our forebears slaved;

☐ eating a sandwich of matzoh, bitter herbs and *charoset*, as per the tradition of the great Jewish scholar, teacher and leader, Hillel, of Second Temple times.

The great Seder meal is then served. Naturally, no leavened products are used, but the talents and ingenuity of Jewish women over the ages have created delicious special Passover foods that satisfy the most finicky palates. Many families have their traditional dishes and recipes that become an integral part of the heritage shared between the generations.

The Seder contains many songs in its ritual. The melodies for these songs vary from one Jewish community to another and even from one family to another. These songs and melodies remain firmly ensconced in the memory of the Jew, individually and collectively, and serve to reinforce the nostalgia and sense of history that is an integral part of our heritage.

54 Sefirah

The period between Passover and Shavuot is devoted to the fulfillment of the Biblical *mitzvah* of counting the days of the Omer. In Biblical times, this period culminated in the bringing of a special grain offering to the Holy Temple in Jerusalem. For forty-nine days, Jews today still count the days that separated our forefathers from their Egyptian Exodus to the defining moment of Jewish tradition, the Revelation at Mount Sinai. Originally, this period of anticipation and commemoration was a happy and satisfying period of the Jewish calendar year. But over the past 1,900 years, this period of time has taken on somber overtones due to national tragedies that have befallen us during these months of springtime and hoped-for renewal.

The first tragedy that is associated with this period of counting, known as *sefirah*, occurred at the time of the Bar Kokhba rebellion against Rome c.135 CE. This four-year long bloody struggle marked the last Jewish attempt to throw off the yoke of Roman occupation of the Land of Israel and its oppressive domination of the Jewish people. The great Rabbi Akiva had supported the rebellion and originally saw Simon Bar Kokhba, the leader of the rebellion, as a potentially messianic figure. But he soon became disillusioned with Bar Kokhba, and the rebellion was crushed by the Romans after a brutal struggle. Rabbi Akiva himself was arrested and executed by the Romans, as were other great rabbis of the Mishnah.

The Talmud relates that during this period of time 24,000 of the students and followers of Rabbi Akiva also died. The Talmud cryptically assigns the reason for their deaths to the fact that they did not properly tolerate and honor each other. This tremendous loss of scholars almost eradicated Torah study among the Jewish People and was marked by a cloak of sadness over the days of the *sefirah*, coinciding with the period of time when these deaths took place. Restrictions regarding haircutting, marriage celebrations, entertainment and other forms of levity during this period now entered Jewish law and practice. Only on Lag B'Omer, the thirty-third day of the count, when the deaths of Rabbi Akiva's disciples ceased, are these restrictions suspended.

In 1096, the Catholic Church embarked upon the First Crusade to free the Holy Land from Moslem rule. There were many reasons that justified the Crusade in the eyes of the leaders of the Church and sovereigns of Europe. Some of them may have been sincerely religious in origin, while other motivations were certainly political, social and economic in nature. In any event, the lure of adventure, booty and the Church's promise of absolution and Paradise to those participating were sufficient incentive for the thousands that joined the ranks of the Crusaders. As the Crusader armies formed in Europe to begin their trek to the Holy Land, they first indulged themselves in an orgy of bloodletting against the local Jewish populations. After all, an infidel is an infidel, wherever one can be found. The great Jewish communities of Worms, Speyers and Mainz were destroyed in the months of April and May 1096 by the rampaging Crusader rabble. Other Jewish communities in France, Germany, Alsace and the

Rhineland were also decimated. All of this blood flowed during the *sefirah* period of time, thus adding more sadness to the burden of those weeks in Jewish history.

In 1648, during the outbreak of Bogdan Chmielnicki's Ukranian revolution against the Polish feudal lords of the time, hundreds of thousands of Jews in Poland, Ukraine and Lithuania were slaughtered by his troops as well as by the opposing Polish forces. Much of this slaughter took place again during the *sefirah* period. The twentieth of Sivan was later instituted as a fast day in memory of the victims of the massacres of 1648-9. The burden of historical sadness that the time of *sefirah* raised in Jewish consciousness became very heavy.

Perhaps our only consolation is the fact that this period of time also affords Jews the opportunity of fulfilling the Biblical *mitzvah* of counting the days till Shavuot, the time of reliving the Sinai Torah experience. When *sefirah* is over, Jewish weddings and celebrations begin once again and we enter upon the summer months with renewed hope.

55 Lag B'Omer

One of the minor holidays in the Jewish calendar year is the eighteenth day of the month of Iyar, a day that corresponds always to the thirty-third day of the counting of the *sefirah*, the seven-week period between Passover and Shavuot. This day of Lag B'Omer (literally, 33 days in the count of the Omer) is noted by the relaxation of the prohibitions on weddings, haircuts, music and public entertainment which otherwise mark the period of the *sefirah*. It is also a day of celebration, of sports and outdoor activities, bonfires and good cheer.

The causes for celebrations on this day have very ancient roots in Jewish history and custom. Joshua fasted on the eighteenth of Iyar, which was the day he led the successful Israelite attack on the Canaanite fortress city of Ai. Thus the day was originally known in Jewish life as the "Fast of Joshua." The eighteenth of Iyar was also the day that the Israelites, who had left Egypt a little more than a month earlier on the fifteenth day of Nissan, finally realized that they were no longer in danger of being pursued by the Egyptian army and that their freedom from Pharaoh's bondage was complete. It was also the day that manna — the heavenly food that sustained the Jews in the desert of Sinai for forty years — began to fall. Thus the day was part of positive Jewish memory from the beginning of the national history of our People.

However, it took on greater importance in the aftermath of the failed Jewish war against Rome and the destruction of the Temple in Jerusalem in 70 CE, and the crushing of the Bar Kokhba rebellion by later Roman legions in 139 CE. The great rebellion against Roman rule by the Jewish Zealots began on the eighteenth of Iyar in the year 63 CE. In the later time of the Bar Kokhba rebellion, 24,000 students and followers of Rabbi Akiva, one of the original supporters of Bar Kokhba, died between Passover and Shavuot. Jewish tradition from the times of the Geonim (sixth century and later Babylonian leaders and scholars) stated that these deaths ended on the eighteenth of Iyar — Lag B'Omer. Thus the day became one of comfort and solace, and hence the relaxation of the restrictions of the solemn *sefirah* laws for that day.

It became customary for Jewish children to go out into the fields and shoot arrows for sport, as a remembrance of the great and nearly successful rebellion of Bar Kokhba and Rabbi Akiva. In modern times, this custom evolved into engaging in hikes, games and outdoor sporting activities. Almost all Jewish schoolchildren, the world over, commemorate the day in this athletic fashion, with Lag B'Omer field trips now popular throughout Jewish society.

The eighteenth of Iyar is also, by the tradition of some rabbinic scholars but not all, the date of the death of Rabbi Shimon bar Yochai. This great Jewish leader was a disciple of Rabbi Akiva, and one of the leaders of the stricken Jewish world (after the failure of the Bar Kokhba rebellion) to reestablish Jewish independence in the Land of Israel. He is also reputed to be the father of kabbalistic studies among Jews and many hold him to be the author of the *Zohar* — the basic book of *Kabbalah*. His fame as a holy man and powerful leader of Torah and spirituality has survived all generations. In commemoration of his death — really of his life — hundreds of thousands of Jews gather on Lag B'Omer at his reputed burial site in Meron, located in the upper Galilee. It has become customary to light large bonfires on the night of Lag B'Omer there, to symbolize the light and warmth of Torah. This custom of lighting bonfires on Lag B'Omer spread throughout the Jewish world. Though there has been much rabbinic disapproval of the bonfires voiced over the ages (based upon the prohibition of the Torah forbidding needless waste or destruction), the custom has persisted.

Associated with Lag B'Omer is also the custom of giving young Jewish boys their first haircut after their third birthday on this day. As on all such days of note in Jewish history, the Jewish People relish the customs and traditions that preserve the memory and the flavor of this notable day on our calendar.

Shavuot:
56 A Sleepless Night

One of the customs of the Shavuot holiday is that of *mishmar*: staying up part or all of the night of Shavuot to study Torah. This custom is based upon the *Midrash* that on the morning when the Jewish People were destined to receive the Torah at Mount Sinai — the first Shavuot in Jewish history — Moses had to rouse them from their sleep to be on time for the historic event. Because they overslept that first Shavuot morning, the people decided that in atonement for that sleepy negligence, henceforth they would spend the night of Shavuot studying Torah and thus be prepared for holiday prayer at the crack of dawn. This custom has become hallowed through the ages, especially in the yeshivot and *batei midrash* (study halls). It is also widely observed today in many synagogues, and there are many interesting and varied classes, forums and discussion groups, all based on Torah subjects, that take place throughout the Jewish world on Shavuot night.

The custom was formalized into the ritual texts of the Jewish People through the editing and publishing of *Tikkun Leil Shavuot*, an established order of study for the night of Shavuot. The *Tikkun* consists of portions of the Bible, Mishnah, Talmud and other works of Torah in synopsis that form a pattern of study for the night. This *Tikkun* appeared in various forms during the early Middle Ages and has been improved upon and expanded over the centuries. It is usually recited by Jews in their synagogues or homes and takes about three hours to read completely.

The Book of Ruth, which is traditionally associated with the holiday of Shavuot, also became a focal point of study on Shavuot night. Currently, there are many rabbis who teach classes throughout the night, and the custom of staying up and learning Torah the entire night of Shavuot is now observed throughout the Jewish world with increasing popularity and diversity. It is again a testimony to the innate love of Torah that is part of the Jewish psyche and soul.

In the past and currently, a *mishmar* — staying up all night to study Torah — is observed weekly on Thursday nights in many yeshivot. And there is always a select group of yeshivah students — *matmidim* — who study Torah well into the late night, even till early morning hours, every day of the year.

The Talmud teaches us that, "the night was created for Torah study." It was therefore commonplace in Eastern Europe and in the Sephardic lands for men to come to study Torah nightly in the synagogues and communal study halls, even after the labors of a hard day's toil. This practice continues today wherever there are Jews committed to the study of Torah. Jews are accustomed to saying that, "there will be plenty of time to sleep in the grave," and therefore whatever free time (usually at night) is available for the study of Torah, the recitation of Psalms or the reading of ethical treatises should be so used. One could say that, challenging as it is, Torah study has been regarded as the recreation and joyous leisure time activity of the Jews worldwide over the millennia. It is no wonder that Torah scholarship has always been regarded as the highest yet most accessible activity possible for every Jew.

In Jerusalem on Shavuot night, beginning at about 3:30 AM, there is an enormous procession of people walking towards the Western Wall in the Old City, to participate in the holiday prayers at sunrise. Even if you wanted to sleep through all Shavuot night in Jerusalem, you could not help be awakened by the steady sound of thousands of marching feet and the murmurs of conversation that accompany this informal procession. The sunrise prayer service attracts tens of thousands of worshippers and is the highlight of the holiday in the Holy City. This assemblage of tens of thousands of Jews at the Western Wall on Shavuot is a reaffirmation of our faith and of our renewed commitment to the Torah given to us at Sinai over 3,300 years ago. Truly, "*Am Yisrael chai*," the People of Israel lives on.

57 Cheese and Flowers

The holiday of Shavuot is singular on the calendar of Jewish holidays. Unlike all other Jewish holidays, it has no special *mitzvot*, nor does it possess a unique holiday presence. Perhaps this is one of the reasons why Shavuot has become almost a forgotten holiday for many in the Jewish world. Yet Shavuot is one of the three major holidays proclaimed in the Torah. It is the anniversary of the Revelation at Sinai and of the giving of the gift of Torah to the Jewish People. In the Torah, we find the holiday of Shavuot described as the holiday of *bikurim* — the bringing of the first fruits of the year's crop to the Temple in Jerusalem. After the destruction of the Holy Temple and the entry into our long exile, the Jewish people could no longer bring *bikurim* to the Temple. Yet they refused to leave the holiday of Shavuot unadorned of distinctiveness. Shavuot was invested by the Jewish People with customs and rituals that have preserved the beauty and uniqueness of the holiday to our day.

One of those customs is eating dairy food at the holiday meal. This is an exception to the general rule that holiday joy requires meat and wine. Shavuot cheesecake and cheese blintzes have become beloved and fattening staples in Jewish homes for centuries. The origins of this custom are grounded in the commemoration of the receiving of the Torah on this day. The Torah itself is compared to milk — "Honey and milk under your tongue" — and thus dairy products are symbolic of that great day at Mount Sinai. After receiving the Torah, the Jewish People could not eat meat immediately, since they had just received the laws of the ritual of animal slaughter and the dietary laws. Hence they ate only dairy products on the day of Revelation, the holiday of Shavuot. A further source of the custom of dairy foods lay in the description in the Torah of the Land of Israel as being "a land that flows with milk and honey." Thus, the dairy foods remind the Jewish People not only of the Torah given at Sinai, but also of our beloved homeland, the Land of Israel.

Another Shavuot custom arose, that of decorating one's home, the synagogue and even the Torah scroll itself with greens and flowers in honor of the holiday. This custom of flowers and greens was based upon a Midrashic statement that the foot of Mount Sinai, where the Jews stood in awe awaiting the granting of the Torah, was carpeted with greens and sweet scented flowers. Even in Eastern Europe, where Jews in the main lived in squalor and poverty, flowers adorned their synagogues on Shavuot. The custom remains strong among Jews today.

So on Shavuot, enjoy the flowers and the cheesecake. Revel in the fact that the Lord has entrusted us the Torah and through it, the task of creating a better world for us and for all mankind.

The Seventeenth
of Tamuz

58

The Seventeenth of Tamuz is one of the four fast days on the Jewish calendar. (Yom Kippur is not counted as a day of fasting but rather as a day of Sabbath-like rest.) This fast day commemorates the breaching of the walls of Jerusalem by the Roman legions in the year 70 CE, as a prelude to their destruction of the Holy Temple three weeks later, on the Ninth of Av. The fast day of the Seventeenth of Tamuz begins the period of time known as the "Three Weeks," a time of introspection and sadness during which numerous prohibitions on personal pleasure and public merry-making reinforce the somber mood. It was this very observance of mourning over the destruction of Jerusalem and the Temple that kept the flame of longing for the Land of Israel lit throughout the long centuries of Jewish Exile.

The Seventeenth of Tamuz has an older history to it than that of the Romans breaching the walls of Jerusalem. According to Biblical and rabbinic tradition, the Seventeenth of Tamuz was the day that Moses descended from Mount Sinai bearing the two tablets of stone upon which were inscribed the Ten Commandments. As he descended from the mountain, he saw the Israelites dancing around the Golden Calf idol and engaging in revelry and immorality. He thrust the tablets of stone from his hands and they were smashed on the ground at the foot of Mount Sinai. The Golden Calf was then destroyed, as were thousands of its Jewish worshippers. This sad day in Jewish history, the punishment for which has played a part in all events of later Jewish history, was thus set aside for reflection well before the Roman legions were on the scene. However, this day did not come into its own as a fast day until the Roman destruction of Jerusalem.

The Seventeenth of Tamuz reminds us that the abandonment of Jewish values and tradition (which is what the Golden Calf represented, and which later led to the destruction of Jerusalem and our national sovereignty) leads to grave national and personal consequences. This day of introspection and memory, the Seventeenth of Tamuz, should not be allowed to slip by in our lives unnoticed and unobserved. If observed now — and if its lessons are engraved on our hearts — eventually, this day, like all of our days of mourning, will be restored as a day of joy and happiness for all of Israel and mankind.

59 The Three Weeks

The period of time between the Seventeenth of Tamuz and the Ninth of Av marks the saddest days of the Jewish calendar year. As discussed previously, the Seventeenth of Tamuz marks the date when the Roman legions breached the walls of Jerusalem in the year 70 CE. It is therefore observed as one of the four fast days of the year. The Ninth of Av marks the date of the destruction of both Temples in Jerusalem, by the Romans in 70 CE and by the Babylonians 490 years earlier. It is observed as a fast day with all of the stringencies of Yom Kippur applied to it. Thus the two fast days of the Seventeenth of Tamuz and the Ninth of Av are the bookends, so to speak, of the "Three Weeks" — the period of remembrance and mourning that is part of the Jewish calendar and Jewish life.

In commemoration of this time of mourning, the Jewish world has adopted a number of ritual laws that are meant to lend personal meaning and significance to this time period. Our rabbis realized long ago that there would be no possibility of maintaining Jewish memory and identity without a framework of ritual and law. Ritual is the container that holds the precious contents of Jewish thought, scholarship and values. Without such a container, the great contents of our faith eventually would be lost. During the "Three Weeks," which is meant to build Jewish memory of the past and strengthen us in the present and the future, there are a number of prohibitions designed to impress upon us the sober reality of the Exile from Zion that has been forced upon us. These concrete acts crystallize the meaning of our loss far more effectively than mere intentions to remember or memorialize.

During the "Three Weeks" no weddings take place, nor do we participate in events of pure entertainment such as musical concerts. New clothes and major house furnishings are not purchased during this period of time, nor are major house refurbishing projects begun. Even partaking of new summer fruits for the first time this year, which according to Jewish law requires a special blessing of *Shehechiyanu* (that "we have been preserved alive to this time"), is avoided.

The "Three Weeks" include the period of time known as the "Nine Days." This block of time begins on the first day of Av and ends with the fast day of the Ninth of Av. During this period of time, the sense of mourning is intensified, as ritual requires that no meat meals be consumed, with the exception of the meals of the Sabbath day or of meals celebrating special occasions such as a *brit* or *Pidyon HaBen*. Recreational swimming and bathing are also avoided during these nine days, and in general the mood in the Jewish world is most somber.

It was exactly these practices and observances that allowed Jews to remember and long for Zion and Jerusalem throughout the long Exile wherever they lived. The return of the Jewish People to the Land of Israel and the establishment of a Jewish State there in our time is a testament to the effectiveness of the rituals of the "Three Weeks" and the "Nine Days" in preserving the attachment of the Jewish People to our ancient past and homeland. Yet the fact that the Jewish People are once again living in the Land of Israel does not negate the mourning of the Ninth of Av and its corollary fast days. The Temple has not been rebuilt, our estrangement from God that caused the Temples' destructions has not been rectified, and vast numbers of Jews are still living in other lands. There is yet a long way to go before the Ninth of Av will be transformed into a national day of joy.

The "Sabbath of Stark Vision": Shabbat Chazon

special reading from the Prophets, a *haftorah*, is read publicly in the synagogue on the Sabbath day that precedes the fast day of the Ninth of Av. The fast day is a day of mourning and repentance marking the destruction of the two Temples in Jerusalem, as well as the defeat of the Bar Kokhba rebellion against Rome in 139 CE, the expulsion of the Jews from Spain in 1492 and other tragedies in Jewish history which coincided with that fateful date. The special *haftorah* reading is taken from the first chapter of the book of Isaiah and is a scathing indictment of the moral failings of Israel. The reading begins with the word *Chazon* — vision. It is from this word that the Sabbath itself derives its special name, *Shabbat Chazon,* the "Sabbath of Stark Vision."

Even though the prophecy of Isaiah was annunciated by him in First Temple times, a century before the actual destruction of the Temple by the Babylonians, it remains uncomfortably and eerily relevant to all other times of

Jewish and human life. The language and words of the prophet have a cruel beauty to them and the list of sins enumerated therein is long. But the central message of the vision is that the Lord expects us to be loyal to Him, to His Torah and to His value system. Tragedy in Jewish history is always traced not only to external factors, but also to spiritual failings and disloyalty among the Jews themselves. The rabbis of the Talmud attributed the destruction of the Second Temple not so much to Roman imperial policy as to the presence of baseless hatred and demonization of others among the Jews themselves. Thus it is not only the historical event that is being remembered: Just as importantly, the spiritual and social cause for that tragic event is highlighted and emphasized.

The normal joy of Sabbath is therefore subdued somewhat on *Shabbat Chazon*. It is a time for introspection and reflection. Jewish law even suggests that festive Sabbath clothing should not be worn on this Sabbath. However, Jewish communal custom remains that even on this Sabbath, as on all other Sabbath days of the year, special Sabbath clothing is nevertheless worn. During the week of the Ninth of Av (according to Sephardic custom) or from the first day of the month of Av onwards (according to Ashkenazic custom), Jews refrain from eating meat or poultry and from drinking wine until after the Ninth of Av. However, on the Sabbath, even on this semi-somber Sabbath, the traditional Sabbath menu, which includes meat dishes as well as wine, is maintained. The Sabbath *zemirot* — songs sung at the Sabbath table — are sung on this Sabbath as well.

Yet the *haftorah* read in the synagogue is sung to the mournful melody of the Book of Lamentations, *Meggilat Eicha*, which is chanted on the night of the Ninth of Av. The joyful poem, *Lecha Dodi*, which is always sung to happy melodies to usher in the Sabbath on Friday nights, is sung on this Sabbath to a much more mournful melody. Thus, this Sabbath of Stark Vision, like much of life itself, is made up of different, oftentimes contradictory customs, ceremonies and emotions.

Even though much of this Sabbath contains overtones of foreboding and sadness, it also carries with it hope and comfort. In order to support this more optimistic view of the future — and Judaism is nothing if not optimistic about mankind's eventual future — Jewish custom ordains that the public reading of Isaiah's dark prophecy end with words of comfort taken from one of his later prophecies. It is certainly true that the stark vision of Isaiah has come to pass in all its horror. But as Rabbi Akiva pointed out long ago in the Talmud, just as the dire prophecies have been fulfilled fully and literally, so too will the prophecies of hope and comfort, of peace and serenity, see full fulfillment and fruition as well.

61 **The Ninth of Av**

There are sad days in the histories of all peoples. Yet these days are rarely commemorated in a big way, for few people are willing to recall and memorialize defeat. Victories and triumphs are days of commemoration, of bands and marches and inspiring speeches. What can one do to commemorate defeat and loss? And in many instances, the day of defeat was a day of finality — there was no national entity left to commemorate the date. But, as in many other ways, the Jewish People is different in this respect too. The Jewish People is an eternal people and therefore the Jewish calendar, which includes days of triumph such as Passover, Chanukah and Purim, also focuses on days of defeat. The day that is therefore the saddest of all days on the Jewish calendar is the ninth day of Av.

This day marks the destruction of both the First Holy Temple (by the Babylonians) and the Second Holy Temple (by the Romans). We also recall the crushing of the Jewish rebellion led by Shimon Bar Kokhba against Roman rule in 139 CE. The Ninth of Av is also the day that the spies sent by Moses to tour the Land of Israel returned to the desert camp of the Israelites and announced their unwarranted negative and pessimistic report. The Jewish People wept that night of the Ninth of Av needlessly, out of a lack of faith in God's ability to bring them to the Promised Land. Therefore, the Lord saw to it that the night of the Ninth of Av would remain a night of weeping for the Jews, but unfortunately it would be so for just cause.

In later Jewish history, the Ninth of Av continued to retain its sinister nature. The expulsion decree issued by King Ferdinand and Queen Isabella that ended over eight centuries of vibrant and productive Jewish life in Spain went into effect on the Ninth of Av in 1492. It was also the day Christopher Columbus left his Spanish port and began his fateful journey to discover the New World. It is ironic that this black day for Spanish Jewry would also, in God's plan of things, somehow bring about the discovery of the continent that would provide a safe haven for Jews in the nineteenth and twentieth centuries.

In 1914, the Ninth of Av saw the beginning of the great battles between Russia and the Central Powers in Central and Eastern Europe. This part of the military campaigns of World War I effectively destroyed the infrastructure of Jewish life in Poland, Lithuania, Byelorussia, Ukraine and Russia. The Bolshevik Revolution, the ensuing Russian Civil War and the virulent anti-Semitism of the postwar nations of Eastern Europe were all precursors of the Holocaust twenty years later. Thus the Ninth of Av continued to serve as a lodestone of sad events and national tragedy for Israel.

During the Holocaust, the Germans picked that day to perform particularly diabolical acts of cruelty against the hapless Jewish populations in their grip. Though there may be other days of sadness for Jews in our long history, there is no day as consistently bleak as the Ninth of Av.

Jews go into full mourning on the Ninth of Av, emphasizing penitence and fasting for twenty-five hours. Seated on the floor or low chairs as mourners, they refrain from wearing leather shoes or bathing, abstain from marital relations and maintain a somber demeanor throughout the day. The Book of Lamentations, *Meggilat Eicha*, is read publicly in the synagogue to a dirge-like melody. At this time the covering tapestry in front of the Torah Ark is removed and the lights in the synagogue are dimmed. *Kinot* — prayers and poems of sadness — are recited at length in the synagogue. The sadness of the day becomes palpable through the ritual forms and symbols of mourning that Jewish tradition has ascribed to the day. It is by these means of symbol and ritual that the Jewish attachment to the Land of Israel and Jerusalem was preserved through nineteen centuries of exile from the land.

The Jewish prophets foresaw this tragedy, yet they also predicted that the long Exile from Zion (and from our previously close connection to God) would someday end during the Messianic era. Thus the Ninth of Av also represents God's promise for redemption and restoration. As in all of our history, sadness and hope commingle, and we arise from our mourning with yet greater confidence and faith in our future.

National Memorial
62 Days

The experience of the Jewish People in exile under Christian and Moslem domination has been a sad and bloody one. Numerous events of horror and the murder of many innocents have marked our path through history. The Jewish people attempted to give meaning to these tragic events and to remember their victims by establishing memorial days that would perpetuate the significance of the event and of its victims. However, the unceasing persecution of Jews throughout the centuries raised the problem that if every act of anti-Jewish violence were to be memorialized, then every day of the year would have to be declared a memorial day. Jewish custom and tradition limits the days of sad memories to a relative few, scattered throughout the calendar year.

In the year 1171, Jews in the French town of Blois were falsely accused of killing a Christian child and using its blood for Passover matzot — one of the earliest incidents of the infamous "blood libels" that stalked Jews for centuries. Approximately 35 Jewish men, women and children, nearly the entire Jewish population of the town, were burned at the stake for the alleged crime on the 20th day of the Hebrew month of Sivan. The Jewish world commemorated this atrocity by specifying the twentieth of Sivan as a fast day and day of remembrance. It became a fixed mark on the Jewish calendar, signifying the poignant victimization of the Jews in hostile surroundings.

In 1648 and 1649, Bogdan Chmielnicki led the Ukranian revolt against the dominance of Poland and Lithuania in the Ukraine. The revolution soon degenerated into the greatest pre-Holocaust pogrom against Jews since the destruction of the Temple in Jerusalem. Approximately 250,000 Jews were brutally slaughtered during this reign of terror. The rabbis of the time decided to memorialize the event by adding it to the pre-existing memorial day for the Jews of Blois, the twentieth day of Sivan. Even though the latter tragedy of 1648-9 far outweighed the earlier massacre of three dozen Jews of Blois in the twelfth century, it was deemed better to combine the memorial of the tragedies on one day, rather than add an additional sad day to the Jewish calendar.

This policy of minimizing the number of days of commemoration of sad events became accepted practice throughout the Jewish world until the Holocaust. However, the enormity of the tragedy of the Holocaust subsumed everything that preceded it in the story of the Jewish People in the Diaspora. The Israeli Knesset, over fifty years ago, decided that the twenty-eighth day of the Hebrew month of Nissan should be designated as Holocaust Remembrance Day. That date is honored in the State of Israel by a wailing siren, a moment of public silence and Holocaust memorial programs conducted at the Yad Vashem Holocaust Museum annually.

Nevertheless, the long-standing rabbinic policy of minimizing the number of days of tragic remembrances played a role in assigning Holocaust remembrance to the Tenth of Tevet for a large section of the Israeli population. That day commemorates the beginning of the destruction of Jerusalem twenty-five centuries ago. The combining of the commemoration of the destruction of European Jewry with the destruction of Jerusalem infers a significant message: Were it not for the sinful behavior of the Jews in Temple times, Jerusalem would never have been destroyed and the Jewish People would not have been dispersed among the many nations of the world, vulnerable to every cruelty. While this concept does not exonerate the victimizers, it implies a spiritual root to centuries of physical suffering. For this reason, for the religiously and historically minded, remembrance would only be meaningful if accompanied by fasting, an indication of repentance.

The principle of combining these days of mourning had been well established well before the Holocaust. The horrible destruction of the Jewish communities of Worms, Speyers and Mainz by the Crusaders in 1096 has long been remembered in the lamentation prayers of the Ninth of Av fast day, even though that destruction actually took place in the months of Iyar and Sivan. The event was originally commemorated in Sivan. We can only look forward to a day in the future when we will only commemorate days of goodness and brotherhood.

Character Refinement

*J*udaism is not a religion of only ritual and prayer. It is one of character development and self-improvement. There are supreme values in Jewish life and there rests an obligation upon Jews to develop within themselves traits of kindness, goodness, self-discipline and optimism. In the nineteenth century, the great Lithuanian sage and rabbi, Yisrael Lipkin of Salant, created a movement called Mussar (literally, ethics, self-chastisement) to promote the goals of positive Jewish character development. Almost every yeshivah and seminary in the Jewish world today devotes part of its curriculum to Mussar. It is much easier to pray and observe ritual than it is to break bad habits or restructure harmful emotions or character traits. In fact, Rabbi Yisrael Lipkin said that, "The loudest noise that can be made in the universe is that of the breaking of a bad habit."

The Torah therefore poses for us absolute goals of character attainment and stresses some basic values and attitudes that are to serve us as our guides in our struggle to become better persons. There are many attitudes and values to discuss in this vein, but I have chosen only four specific values to form this section of the book: Subduing Anger; Kindness; Justice; and Truth. The truth is that, in my opinion, all of the *other possible values and attitudes that I could have listed here are in reality only corollaries to these basic traits and values. The rabbis of the Mishnah have taught us that, "The work is great...and one has no right to desist from accomplishing its goals; but nevertheless the Lord does not expect us to fully complete the task." That aphorism is certainly true as regards character building. The goals remain very high and the attempt to achieve them is a lifelong struggle. Even if we do not complete the task, we are not freed of the obligation to try.*

63 **Subduing Anger**

n his great works of Jewish thought, Maimonides advocates following "the golden mean" by seeking balance and avoiding extremism in all character traits. One should not be overly miserly with money, nor should one squander it or spend it uninhibitedly. Speech should be careful and measured; eating habits should be sensible; cleanliness is necessary, but it should not be obsessive. In the entire gamut of human behavior, he maintains, Judaism advocates normalcy. Yet he postulates that there are two exceptions to this rule of balance.

The exceptions are humility and the avoidance of anger. In those areas one is allowed, in fact bidden, to go to the extreme. There is no limit to the cultivation of humility, and there is no human trait as destructive as anger. It is no coincidence that these two are limitless. In reality, humility and avoidance of anger are inextricably linked together, for it is our innate arrogance that fuels our feelings of frustration and anger. It is the perceived attack on our ego that is usually at the base of our anger. A truly humble person does not lack self-esteem; he simply feels it is unnecessary to defend his position or honor in every instance.

In anger, a person loses control and often says and does things that are tremendously harmful. They are usually irrevocable in the damage that they inflict. The rabbis of the Talmud taught us that all the instances of angry outbursts described in the Bible "left an impression." Even the great Moses, the humblest of all humans, is recorded as becoming angry with the Jewish People over their errant behavior and rebelliousness (imagine that!) and was punished by God for his actions and speech due to that anger. The great Hillel is renowned in the Talmud not so much for his enormous erudition and scholarship as for his ability to control all feelings of anger within himself, no matter how severely provoked. The wise rabbis of the Talmud said that one could recognize the true nature of another person by judging that individual's capacity to control anger; and they had little tolerance for angry people, even when it was claimed that in their anger they espoused and promoted righteous causes.

There is a great difference between true righteous indignation and anger. We have the right and duty to be indignant over wrongs and wrongdoing. But anger is a passion that controls us, that takes over our entire being, that makes us lose all sense of proportion and perspective. Angry words hurled during an argument in a family, school or work setting leave scars that never fully heal. I have witnessed awful behavior by otherwise fine and sensible people when they were overcome by a fit of anger. It is not a pleasant experience.

What practical means can be employed to deal with our feelings of anger? Once when I was on the verge of succumbing to angry feelings and expressions, my father-in-law, of blessed memory, told me that he had worked for seven years to overcome the trait of anger. And it is true that I never saw him angry in the forty years that we were together in life. He explained to me that he once witnessed an instructive conversation in the house of the great Rabbi Yisrael Meir Kagan, known as the Chafetz Chaim, one of the most revered and beloved leaders of Eastern European Jewry of the early twentieth century. There were visitors in the house annoying the rabbi and truly provoking him. My father-in-law saw the great man withdraw from the conversation, go to a corner of the room and converse with *himself*. "Yisrael Meir," he said, "why are you becoming angry? Will anger help you? Will it accomplish anything?" After a few minutes of such self-conversation, he returned to his visitors, calm and in control of his emotions, and the discussion ended quietly and peacefully.

I have tried this exercise myself numerous times. It works, it really does. Try it.

64 Kindness

This character trait is rendered in Hebrew as *gemilut chasadim*. In its broadest sense, this means extending one's self on behalf of the welfare of others. It is wide ranging in both scope and activity. The concept includes, but certainly is not limited to, extending hospitality to guests in one's home, whether the guests are relatives (maybe especially if they are relatives!) or complete strangers; visiting the sick and providing for their needs and the needs of their families; burying the dead in an honorable and proper fashion; being charitable with one's time, attention and funds; consoling the bereaved; and exhibiting a kindly, friendly, cheerful disposition to all those with whom we come in contact. In its broadest sense, *gemilut chasadim* represents an attitude of service to others and an emulation of the ways of God. It is one of the basic pillars upon which all of Jewish society — in fact, all human society — rests.

The trait of kindness towards others, all kinds of others, is an inheritance from the founders of the Jewish

People, Abraham and Sarah. God's ways are too inscrutable and difficult for us to truly know and imitate, so Abraham and Sarah are regarded as our human role models of the ways of kindness. It is known that their tent was open on all sides so that all wayfarers could enter easily and without delay. Hospitality extended to strangers and the unfortunate, and concern for others — even when those others were undeserving — characterized their home. We, as their descendants, are bound by tradition, history and covenant to follow in their ways of kindness. For centuries, it has been the mark of Jewish culture wherever Jews may be found in the world.

Kindness always has to be tempered by good sense. "Killing with kindness" is not just an ironic phrase; it is a true danger. In Judaism there are strict restraints as to the timing and propriety of exhibitions of kindness. Visiting the sick must be done with caution and wisdom. And even when it is proper and desirable to visit the sick, never overstaying one's welcome becomes the ultimate kindness. This is especially true when serious or painful situations are involved. In my years as a congregational rabbi, I was almost a daily visitor at the local hospitals to visit congregants or members of my community. The most heartfelt thanks that I received from patients after their recovery was to thank me for making the hospital visit to them one that was brief and comforting.

The same rule of restrained kindness applies to visiting and comforting the bereaved. The *shiva* period of bereavement and grief is a halachic method of catharsis and rehabilitation for the person suffering the loss of someone beloved. At such times, some people need company and some people need to be left alone. The true act of kindness is discerning what the mourner needs and accommodating one's visit to that need. The duration of the visit and what is said is a matter of utmost sensitivity and personal feeling.

A little-known rule for the *shiva* visit is that the visitor should not address the mourner until the mourner speaks directly to him or her, and then the subject of conversation should be started by the mourner. The wisdom of this practice is that the mourner is given the chance to express himself or herself as the need is felt and is not subject to the well-intentioned, but possibly erroneous, assumptions of the visitor. The right word is often the greatest kindness that we can offer one to another, as the wrong word, no matter how well intentioned, can hurt. Kindness is always measured by the need of the other and not by the intent (no matter how noble) of the one who believes that he or she is extending kindness.

There are numerous communal kindnesses that have taken the form of organized institutions in our communities. Every Sabbath-observant Jewish community has arrangements for hospitality homes for strangers who may be passing through. Jews stranded unexpectedly over the Sabbath in a strange community can be assured of Sabbath meals (and often, a place to stay) by speaking with the rabbi or by merely attending the synagogue and revealing their plight. Jewish communities maintain a Jewish burial society, almost always manned by volunteers. Proper and dignified burial and care for the bereaved family is called the "ultimate kindness" in Jewish tradition.

Kindness to neighbors and attentiveness to their needs and personalities is emphasized throughout Jewish moral and legal books. Free loan societies that make interest-free monetary loans to the needy abound in the Jewish world. In addition, societies that lend bridal dresses, jewelry, medical supplies, wheelchairs, baby carriages, dinnerware and a host of other goods without charge are fixtures throughout religious Jewish communities all over the world. These loan societies are known by the Hebrew acronym *GemaCH*, which of course is an abbreviation of *gemilut chasadim*, and they are notable in the fact that their goods are dispensed with no shame to the borrower. Kindness in the Jewish world, therefore, is not merely an attribute or a utopian ideal. It is a way of life.

65 Justice

Justice in Jewish thought and life is not an abstract goal but is rather a practical method of solving problems and disputes between human beings. The statue of the blindfolded goddess of justice atop the U.S. Supreme Court building is not quite the symbol that Judaism would use. That blindfold is meant to convey the impartiality of the justices and the court, and their freedom from being influenced by those who appear before them. Judaism is certainly in agreement with that idea. In fact that idea is Biblical in origin and the Torah expresses itself numerous times on the necessity of not favoring the rich and influential or the poor and downtrodden in deciding issues being litigated.

However, Jewish thought objects to the notion that justice is "blind." A Jewish court must recognize whatever special circumstances pertain to the case and its decision must be tailored to this particular instance. Justice has to deal with real people and not only with abstract laws and theories. In Judaism, justice is a practicality, not a philosophical ideal. In the eyes of Judaism, judges must not only be scholars versed in the law, but just as importantly they must be people of common sense, worldly experience and human insight. Legal scholars can "put an elephant through the eye of a needle," if necessary. But rarely does that produce justice. A broad view and a true focus on the people involved will always create a feeling of genuine justice between the disputants themselves and in the eyes of society at large.

Judaism always warns against strict legalism in attempting to achieve justice. The Bible warned us that, "In the place of the law, [there] one can find the place of evil." It speaks of "creating oppression and crookedness by law." It opposes narrow interest justice that would impair society, even though technically correct. It demands a higher sense of justice from the judges and the litigants than the literal fulfillment of the rule of law itself.

The Talmud tells us of a great rabbi who hired workers to move barrels of wine and the workers broke some of those barrels. The rabbi confiscated the street clothing that they had left with him for safekeeping after they had changed into their work clothes, in order to ensure that his damages would be paid. The workers appealed to the rabbinical court for the return of their garments. The rabbi/judge ordered the employer to return the street wear to the workers. The rabbi asked the court in wonderment, "Is that the [Torah] law?"

The judge replied, "Yes, that is the law, for you are bidden 'to walk in the ways of the just.'" The workers were vastly encouraged by the judge's decision and now dared to ask for payment of their wages from their employer. The judge again decided in favor of the workers, again explaining his decision as "walk[ing] in the ways of the just." There is a concept in Jewish law called *lifnim meshurat hadin* — doing more than what the written technical law requires. For a great rabbi, such as described in the case of the workers above, the court demanded that he live up to not only the minimum legal standard, but to the greater societal standard of justice for one of his stature. That standard prevails over the narrower, legally and technically correct standard of the law books.

A measure of Jewish justice is determined by the standard of what is appropriate: appropriate to the given instance, appropriate to the general community, appropriate to the entire society, appropriate to the relationship between God and human beings. All of these measures of what is appropriate are linked together in the Jewish concept of justice and all of them are always present in any given case.

The purpose of justice is to advance the cause of mankind and to improve society. It is here to give an impetus of morality to all of human behavior and actions. It is here to transcend the narrow confines of a given case and to establish a society where the value system of "walk[ing] in the ways of just" can take hold and eventually dominate. Ultimately, justice will rise above the confines of the law books and the court chambers, and pervade all sections and members of society.

66 Truth

One of the great enemies of spiritual growth and emotional security is participating in a pattern of falsehoods. People who lie to others, lie to themselves as well. The Torah places great emphasis on truth as a way of life. It warns us that, "One should stay far away from falsehoods."

Maimonides states that the root cause of Jewish opposition to idolatry and paganism is that these ideas are patently false. Thus it is not the idol itself that is so repugnant as is the falseness of that idol. According to Jewish Midrashic tradition, the seal of God, so to speak, is *emet* — truth. The word *emet* is composed of the first, middle and last letters of the Hebrew alphabet. Truth, therefore, has eternity and continuity, in contradistinction to the temporary and, of necessity, ever changing nature of lies.

The rabbis of the Talmud taught us that a lie "has no legs," i.e. that it will not stand up to the tests of time and circumstance. To tell the truth requires only a one-time statement of fact, whereas lies involve us in the necessity for constantly fabricating further lies and cover-ups. The ultimate spiritual and educational goal of Judaism is the search for truth. It is also the wisest, most practical and productive course in life as well.

Truth ennobles all whom it reaches. Lies demean all who unfortunately come in contact with them. Out of all the character traits of humans, truth is an absolute. Something that is 99% true is not really true. Thus the standard of truth is a very high one that defies easy accomplishment and achievement.

Yet, truth can harm and destroy. Many times truth is painful to tell and even more painful to hear. The Torah, which is the paradigm of goodness and practicality, allows for a loophole in the ironclad rule of truth. To help achieve peace and harmony, to avoid unnecessary discord and disruption, under certain circumstances, one is allowed to shade the subject matter somewhat. The Lord Himself, in telling Abraham about Sarah's laughter when the angel told her that she would bear a child at the age of ninety, did not tell him the whole truth. For Sarah had said, "My husband is too old." The Lord did not repeat that remark to Abraham — and in not doing so spared the couple pain and aggravation. The Torah does not condone falsehoods. But it does require that truth, at least in relations with other human beings, be employed as a rapier and not as a broadsword. The excuse of being truthful is often employed as a cover for being cruel. In Jewish life and practice, truth is always tempered by common decency and courtesy towards others.

The great ally in accomplishing this knife-edge balancing act of not lying, while at the same time not slamming home unpleasant truths, is silence. But even while appreciating the difficulties and potential damage that truth entails, one should never give up on the concept of the supremacy of truth at all times and in most circumstances.

Intellectual honesty is the byproduct of the quest for truth. Judaism views plagiarism as out and out stealing. But the goal of intellectual honesty demands more than simply not being a thief. Rashi (Rabbi Shlomo Yitzchaki, eleventh century France), the greatest of the commentators to the Bible and the Talmud, will often write in his commentary when referring to a difficult word or passage in the text: "I do not know its meaning." Rashi did not wish to leave any false impressions as to his scholarship or knowledge. It is his ability to sometimes say, "I don't know" that gives the student full confidence in his explanations and exposition of the text when "he does know."

This in itself serves as a clear example of the long run practical benefit of being truthful and honest. Honesty and truthfulness at home, in the marketplace, in communal affairs and most importantly, to one's self, is the Jewish prescription for meaningful and successful living.

Education

*T*he words of the Talmudic rabbis that "the ignorant can never achieve true piety" form the basis of the Jewish attitude towards education. In a class-oriented and largely unlettered world, Judaism raised the banner of schooling and knowledge for all. The great heroes in Jewish life have always been the people of letters and spirit. Even David, the vaunted ancient king and warrior of Israel, is remembered more for his Psalms than for his victorious battles.

Knowledge is the key that unlocks life for us and therefore Jews possess a reverence for knowledge and education second only to their reverence for life itself. The prime area of Jewish education has always been the written Torah — the Bible, and the Oral Law — the Mishnah and Talmud. I am not aware of any other books in the history of civilization that have been so thoroughly perused, studied, explained, debated and analyzed as the Jews have done to the Hebrew Bible, the Mishnah and the Talmud. And the study of these texts has remained inexhaustible.

Throughout Jewish history, this devotion to Torah study has spilled over into all other areas of knowledge and creative human thought. Medicine, music, philosophy, astronomy, literature and the sciences have also become part of the educational world of Jews. It is estimated that over 80% of

Jewish youth in the United States and over 60% of their contemporaries in Israel attend schools and yeshivot of higher education. This proportion of students attending institutions of higher learning is far and away much higher than the corresponding proportion among the youth of the general population, even in advanced Western countries, let alone the Middle East.

The deep-seated love that Jews possess for the pursuit of knowledge is rooted in a drive that has been implanted within them by many centuries of Torah study and an insatiable longing to master the holy texts. The following section touches upon some of the educational systems, ancient and modern, which have perpetuated this ideal.

67 Schools

nterestingly enough, the Torah makes no reference to schools nor suggests formal systems of educating the populace. It does, however, emphasize in numerous places the duty of parents to educate their children in Torah values, Jewish tradition and life skills. The Mishnah and the Talmud reinforce these Torah ideas with more explicit guidelines as to the range of schooling and the skills and values to be taught, including professional and job training and the ability to swim. But the broader educational system is not really addressed, and the tradition seemingly assumes a system of home schooling or private tutoring. Because the Torah was intended for all time and all cultures, the exact method of instruction is not specified, presumably to allow it to vary from culture to culture.

There is, however, mention in the Talmud that during the First and Second Temple periods there was a general elementary school system in place that extended "from Dan (the northernmost point of Land of Israel) to

Beersheba (the southernmost point)." The Talmud even recommends that the class size in these institutions should never exceed twenty-five students per teacher. Whether home schooling and private tutoring were reserved for the wealthy and the intellectually elite exclusively is not specified in the Talmud, though it can be safely inferred that this was the case. In any event, it seems that the best students progressed to higher schools of Torah — yeshivot — after a period of time, and the others left formal studying to take their place in the marketplace of everyday life.

The Jewish Diaspora centered in Babylonia after the destruction of the Second Temple. There, the system of yeshivot was expanded, at times numbering in the thousands of students. Elementary education remained in the same form as it had been earlier, with much home schooling and local schools for children in elementary grades. The better teachers were hired by the wealthy to tutor their children and this affected the level of competence and education in the local community schools.

In the Middle Ages, both in France and Spain, the Jewish communities relied on home schooling, private tutoring and loosely organized schools to provide Torah education for their young. In Spain, Jews also engaged tutors to teach philosophy, mathematics, natural sciences and literature to their children. Many of the teachers who taught these subjects were non-Jews and this became a divisive issue in Spanish Jewish life, as well as among the Spanish non-Jews. Both groups were afraid of the influence followers of the other religion may have on them. After the Christian domination of Spain took hold, the Church moved to prevent Jews from hiring Christian tutors — or even Christian maids — to serve in their homes.

In Eastern Europe, from the seventeenth century onward, the system of schooling was concentrated in the institution of the *cheder* (literally, a room). The *cheder* was for boys who entered the schoolroom at three years of age and continued their studies until they were ten or eleven. The education received in the *cheder* was uneven, depending on the skill and patience of the *melamed* — the teacher. Much of the rebellion against traditional Jewry in the eighteenth and nineteenth centuries found its roots in the deplorable physical and educational features of the *cheder*. The wealthy and the elite continued to provide home schooling and private tutoring for their children. The boys who showed intellectual promise advanced to learn with the rabbi of the town, and those who shone there were passed on to study with even greater scholars and well-known rabbis. Girls were generally taught at home.

The yeshivah system of today, serving adolescent and young adult men, did not begin in Eastern Europe until the beginning of the nineteenth century. In Chassidic communities, education after the *cheder* years took place in *shtieblach* — small private houses of study and prayer that operated independently of each other, with no fixed schedule or curriculum. Thousands of students frequented these *shtieblach*, which were primarily centers of private, independent study.

Today's Orthodox Jewish education system is based on a day school elementary school education, teaching both Jewish and secular subjects; yeshivah high school, again with instruction in both Jewish and secular subjects; and then advanced Torah study in a men's yeshivah or women's seminary. This latter stage of advanced study is pursued by many young people from all over the Jewish world, often in Israeli institutions of higher learning. There are also a number of religious Jewish universities, which combine higher Jewish studies with advanced secular and professional disciplines in North America and Israel.

Though the American after-school congregational Talmud Torah and Sunday schools are dwindling in number, some still survive. There are also numerous non-Orthodox and communal day schools in America that combine Jewish and secular studies. These day schools have begun to grow in number, as parents and community leaders are more actively seeking to educate their youngsters to ensure Jewish continuity.

68 Yeshivot

The institution of yeshivot is a very ancient one. The *Midrash* states that our patriarchs Abraham, Isaac and Jacob all established yeshivot. Their yeshivot were antedated by the legendary yeshivah of Shem and Eiver, founded by Noah's descendants immediately after the great Flood. These early yeshivot apparently were schools where the ideas of monotheism and Noachide morality were taught. The philosophy of the rejection of idolatry and paganism; the prohibitions against robbery, murder, sexual promiscuity, corrupt systems of justice, cruelty to humans and animals, were all developed and taught in these early yeshivot. Our patriarch Jacob studied for fourteen years in the yeshivah of Shem and Eiver before departing on his road of exile to the house of Lavan in Syria/Iraq. In short, the Talmud sums up the matter in its statement: "Never has study in yeshivot been interrupted from the time of our forefathers."

Great yeshivot existed in the Land of Israel and in Babylonia from the end of the period of the First Temple.

Thousands of students attended these yeshivot. It was in those institutions that the Oral Law of Sinai was written, edited and published after the destruction of the Second Temple. The debates of the great scholars of the Jewish People over a period of seven centuries are recorded in the Mishnah, in the Babylonian Talmud and in the Jerusalem Talmud.

The yeshivot came under fierce persecution from the Greeks, then the Romans and finally from the Byzantine Christians. In fact, virtually all of our enemies over the long centuries of Jewish struggle and exile attempted to destroy the institution of the yeshivah and uproot its goal of devotion to Torah study from the midst of Israel.

And they all have failed in this nefarious effort. From Nebuchadnezzar to Stalin, neither Church nor secular tyrant was able to stifle the love of Torah that exists within the Jewish People and which always found expression in yeshivot.

Most of our current-day yeshivot are modeled on the structure of the famous Yeshivah of Volozhin, the "mother of the (present day) yeshivot." Founded in the early 1800's by Rabbi Chaim, the rabbi of Volozhin (a hamlet in Lithuania), the yeshivah operated for the balance of the century as the training school for the great leaders, scholars, poets and dreamers that later built the modern Jewish world. Volozhin itself spawned many other major yeshivot in Europe, Israel and America, founded by the students of that great institution.

The Volozhin Yeshivah was persecuted ruthlessly by the czarist government. Sadly, there were "enlightened Jewish progressives" who aided and abetted the anti-Semitic Russian government in its attempts to "modernize" the yeshivah and the Jewish People. In 1892, the Russian government closed the yeshivah in Volozhin, but other yeshivot took its place. The czar and his hateful successors, the Communists, are no longer here, but the yeshivot all over the world continue to grow and prosper, socially and spiritually.

Yeshivot today reflect the wide differences that exist within traditional Jewish society. There are Chassidic yeshivot of many different nuances and methods of study, reflecting the ideas of the Chassidic dynasties that sponsor the particular school. There are the "Lithuanian" yeshivot that pattern themselves on the style and curriculum of study of Volozhin and its successors. There are yeshivot that combine vocational training with Torah study, as there are those that incorporate army service (in Israel) within its program. There are yeshivot that provide for a college education and secular degrees and there are those that are devoted solely to Torah study.

The common denominator of all yeshivot is intense Torah and Talmudic studies, a striving for righteousness and a sense of responsibility and leadership for the spiritual welfare of coming generations of Jews. The yeshivot truly remain the creative engine of the Jewish world.

69 Schools for Women

P robably the greatest internal revolution within Jewish life over the past century has been the role of schools and higher Jewish education for women. In early nineteenth century Eastern Europe and in the Sephardic world of the time as well, most Jewish women were barely literate, if not even illiterate. In Eastern Europe, most Jewish women did not attend synagogue services regularly and when they did pray, they did so in *Yiddish* with special prayers — *techinos* (supplications) — not from the regular Hebrew prayer book, the *siddur*. The reasons for these deficiencies in Jewish education for women then were in the main societal. Jews lived in societies where illiteracy was almost universal among women. By the end of the nineteenth century, the situation for women's education was already changing.

From the late nineteenth century onward, significant sections of the Jewish youth were becoming radicalized due to the poverty and persecution that plagued Eastern

European Jewry. While the older generation of Jewish women remained satisfied with their *techinos*, their daughters were becoming rapidly secularized by the movements of change — Socialism, Zionism, secularism, among others — that were then sweeping Eastern European Jewish society. In a famous letter that the Grand Rabbi of Gur wrote in the early 1920's, he described a common situation that on Friday nights, "the father and the son of the family, in Chassidic garb, come to me, while the daughters of the family go to the theater! How can the Jewish home survive under such circumstances?"

For many reasons, the secularization of Jewish women in Eastern Europe proceeded at a faster pace than that of their brothers. It was this threat to the very existence of the traditional Jewish home and family that brought about the great change in women's education in traditional circles

In the early 1920's, a woman by the name of Sarah Schnirer, a seamstress by previous vocation, founded a small girls' school in Cracow, Poland. Originally having only thirteen students, Schnirer's little school started a network of girls' schools throughout Poland that numbered tens of thousands of students barely fifteen years later. The schools were organized as the Bais Yaakov school system. Bais Yaakov (House of Jacob) was the title given to Jewish women at the scene of the Revelation at Sinai. In Lithuania, the parallel school system for girls was called Yavneh. The girls' schools were for young children, adolescents and young adults. After high school, there were women's seminaries for training teachers established throughout Europe.

In the United States, such schools and seminaries did not begin to be popular until after World War II. Today there are tens of thousands of young Jewish women attending Torah schools for women, and there are a number of excellent schools of higher Jewish studies for women that are an integral part of the American Jewish scene.

Essays on Jewish History, Thought and Beliefs

*A*ll faith is based upon certain attitudes and beliefs. These create the value system of the religious society and are the measuring rods by which individual and societal behavior is judged. In Judaism, many of these attitudes and values are translated into commandments and mandatory behavior patterns. But even those that remain in the realm of the spirit and intellect, so to speak, are also ultimately vital to forging the character and soul of the Jew and the human being.

The basic belief of Judaism is that there is a personal God Who fashioned each of us individually and Who is vitally interested in our lives and behavior. Judaism does not accept randomness as an answer to the unfathomable questions of life. Nor does Judaism accept randomness in scientific inquiry, in human behavior or unreasonable tragedy, in the behavior of nations or in the course of history. We believe that the Lord cares about us individually and we care about Him as well.

Because of this basic belief, many attitudes in Jewish life are understandable. Judaism is not a fatalistic religion. Human beings have complete freedom of choice and behavior. Righteousness and wickedness are not preordained. Yet, we are encompassed within a certain boundary of God's

Will that guides us and makes us active players in the story of civilization that is God-driven. Balancing these ideas is the task of Jewish philosophy, but it is no less the task of each and every individual Jew.

The attitudes and beliefs discussed in this next chapter (sometimes framed in historical contexts) are examples of Jewish thought regarding various subjects and situations in life. They illustrate how Judaism plays a constant and central role in all aspects of human life and why it is not only a faith, it is primarily a way of life and living.

70 Jewish Law, Halachah

The Hebrew word *halachah* literally means a path or a way of going. In its broader sense, *halachah* is a description of the fundamental guidepost of Jewish life and behavior. It is the law, traditions and customs of Torah and the nation of Israel as expounded throughout the ages. It presupposes a belief in the Divine origin of the Written Torah and the Oral Law. This extends to the ideas and traditions of the Talmud and the halachic process. The discussions, questions and answers, precedents and flexibility must be within the parameters of the "red lines" that the Torah and the Talmud themselves require. The *halachah* is the development of Jewish life on the basis of the Torah and traditions given by God to Moses at Sinai. As such, it points the way to the primary place of Torah in personal and national Jewish life, as well as providing practical answers to questions of ritual, behavior and policy in Jewish society.

Judaism without the halachic parameters described above becomes an empty shell, a ship that has no anchor in storm-tossed waters. A faith without immutable legal guidelines is unable to provide continuity and identity to its young. Jewish history knows no form of non-halachic Judaism that has survived the vicissitudes of world events for long. That is why adherence to *halachah* remains the pivotal issue in determining the future fate of individual Jewish families and the Jewish People at large.

In the ninth century, Rabbi Saadya Gaon stated the maxim, "Our nation, the Jewish People, is a nation only because of the Torah." By that he meant that it is loyalty to *halachah* and adherence to its precepts and life style that binds the generations of the Jewish People together. This concept has been stressed by all later scholars until our very time. In the State of Israel, Jews of widely varying backgrounds, cultures and origins have successfully united and often melded together due to the common tie they have to Torah.

There are no officially appointed decisors of *halachah*. (I will admit that the term "decisor" is obscure. More than an adjudicator of legal disputes, a "decisor" applies Jewish legal precedent to all questions posed and renders a final decision. The Hebrew term for this person is *posek* — for which there is no English equivalent. The term implies that he is one who ends the legal discussion with a decision, as a period ends a sentence.) Rabbis are naturally charged with answering the halachic questions of their congregants and communities. However, on major ritual and social issues and problems, there have always been great scholars and leaders in every generation who accepted upon themselves the role of being the ultimate national decisors of *halachah* for their time. These great people are known for their scholarship and knowledge, and perhaps even more importantly, for their incorruptibility and personal character.

These experts in Jewish law are charged with the task of giving definitive answers to difficult issues. They are not loophole seekers, nor are they subject to popular will (as sometimes conventional rabbis might be) in deciding these weighty matters. They are well versed in halachic precedents and are aware of existing Jewish public policy toward major issues, and these considerations naturally loom large in their thinking and decisions. In presenting questions to these great decisors, the Jewish People are not asking them to circumvent *halachah*, rather they are to determine the applicable *halachah* itself.

How are they chosen? Somehow there arises a national consensus among the Jewish People that these are the people to whom halachic questions should be addressed. Many times answers vary among decisors. In such cases, events, time and history eventually decide between the opinions advanced. Since all of the opinions of these noted scholars are within the parameters of halachic thought and Jewish belief, one may follow the opinion of the decisor that one feels is correct, until the matter is finally settled by time and majority practice. For example, the last few generations have raised new halachic questions relating to modern technology, appliances, social changes, educational practices, medical ethics, governmental issues in the State of Israel, war and peace, archeological discoveries and the Holocaust. All of these issues, and many more, have been raised by the halachic decisors of the time and have been dealt with, though not always in clear-cut unanimity. *Halachah* is a living instrument that contains the necessary flexibility, within its clear Torah and Talmudic parameters, to deal with all issues of life in all times and circumstances.

It is customary for every Jewish family to have a halachic authority to whom they turn for answers to the questions of life, both great and small. The congregational rabbi, the head of the yeshivah, the Chassidic rebbe, the recognized great scholar of Torah, are all examples of such authorities. In the modern world, personal independence and autonomy reign supreme. To a halachically observant Jew, the presence of such an authority figure, coupled with the discipline of *halachah* in our personal and public lives, serves as a necessary counterweight to the rootless anguish plaguing modern society.

71 Intellectual Honesty

ne of the hallmarks of our great Torah scholars throughout the generations has been the uncompromising loyalty to the concept of intellectual honesty in their writings and commentaries. One would almost take this for granted, for the subject that is being dealt with is *Torat Emet* — the Torah given at Sinai that represents ultimate and eternal truth and honesty. Nevertheless, the temptation to falsify, exaggerate, deny, plagiarize and even commit forgery is a well-known affliction in general academic circles. As such, the unswerving path of intellectual honesty that one finds in the writings of the great Torah scholars of Israel is exemplary and inspiring.

The Talmud is replete with incidents of great people who said, "I was wrong," or "I do not know." In fact, it is the mark of intellectual greatness to be able to retract previously strongly held opinions and to be able to say that one does not know everything. The temptation of scholars, because they do know so much, is to believe that they know everything. They then fall into the trap of leaving no question unanswered and no query ignored.

A great Jewish legend relates that two outstanding scholars, each of whom had written a great work on the same subject of Torah law, once met. One of the books had achieved instant and wide acceptance in the scholarly world while the other lagged far behind, even though its author was equal to his colleague in brilliance and knowledge. The disappointed author asked the other scholar to review with him his daily schedule of study and research. After hearing the routine of his colleague, the man exclaimed: "That is my exact schedule as well, so why is your book so much more popular than mine?" The other man answered: "I neglected to tell you that every night I spend an hour erasing some of what I wrote during the day!" As an erstwhile author, I can testify that it is much simpler to write than to erase one's words.

The champion of Jewish scholarship and therefore of intellectual honesty in matters of Torah scholarship is Rashi — Rabbi Shlomo Yitzchaki. This towering figure in Jewish life lived in France close to one thousand years ago. He composed the inspired commentary to the Bible and the Talmud that has remained the basic commentary to these books of Jewish faith to this very day. For Jews, it is unthinkable to study the Bible or the Talmud without using Rashi's commentary. Yet in forty-four instances Rashi stated in his commentary on the Talmud: "I do not know what this means." Furthermore, in Rashi's commentary to the Bible, he states in seventy-seven instances, "I don't know what this means." Rashi could have just ignored the word, phrase or idea in question and continued with his commentary. But that would not have been intellectually honest, for it would leave the student of Rashi with the impression that the matter was so simple or obvious that it required no explanation. Rashi therefore steps forward and advises us that he does not know the word, phrase or idea that appears in the text and we are therefore warned that there is a problem facing us. That intellectual honesty is what makes Rashi the eternal teacher of the Jewish People.

In the nineteenth century, with the rise of "enlightened" scholars and "Biblical Criticism," the standards of intellectual honesty in the Jewish world were compromised. Books that were out and out forgeries were attributed to great scholars of past ages. Emendations of texts in the Bible and other books of Jewish faith became the rage in the world of "enlightened" Christian and Jewish scholars.

Today, most of these shenanigans have been consigned to the ash heap of history, while Rashi and his colleagues in faith and truth continue to lead the way to a vital understanding of our Torah, its words and its values.

72 **Modesty**

O ne of the strongest and most emphasized values in Jewish life is that of modesty. It has many different areas of application in life. One area is certainly humility of personality. The Talmud lists humility as one of the two areas where extremism is permitted — one should be extremely humble. (The other area is the avoidance of anger at almost all costs.) Arrogance is a personality crime of major proportion. The greatest compliment paid by the Torah to our great master and teacher Moses is that "he was the most humble of all people on the face of this earth." We can truly state that the entry to all other aspects of modest behavior in life is the development of the modest personality within one's self.

Modesty does not mean that one does not recognize one's self-worth, talents and accomplishments. It does mean that even though one may have great abilities and achievements to one's credit, those factors do not give one the right to behave in an arrogant fashion towards others. Our talents are God-given, and it is simply our job to cultivate the abilities He has chosen to invest in us. This does not make us better than anyone else. Humility and modesty of personality enable us to see ourselves in accurate and realistic perspective and help us avoid the terrible trap of arrogance.

Judaism also deals with modesty in speech. Obscenities degrade the great gift that God granted us — the ability to talk and communicate one with another. It is our ability to speak that distinguishes us as humans and not merely another form of species in the animal kingdom. Therefore speech should be treated as a gift given to humans in trust, and not be abused. One of the reasons that Jews call Hebrew the "holy language" is the fact that this language contains no obscene or curse words. In modern-day Hebrew spoken in Israel, all of these unfortunate words and phrases have been imported into the Israeli vernacular from foreign tongues.

Modesty in speech also entails the avoidance of speaking gossip or slander about others. This practice is called *lashon hora*, "bad speech," and is expressly forbidden many times in the Torah. The Talmud saw in all of the protective bodily barriers that guard the tongue — the mouth, lips, teeth and palate — the clear message that the tongue should never be given free rein. Modesty in speech is a Jewish requirement.

Modesty in dress is also part of the makeup of Jewish life. The Torah objects to provocative dress by men or women. There is great latitude in Jewish life to dress in an attractive and fashionable style. Judaism is not a religion of prudishness per se. However, the Torah has a healthy respect for the physical attraction between the sexes.

The Torah sees the intimate physical relationship between men and women as legitimate and desirable, but only within the framework of marriage. Sexual relationships outside of the marriage relationship are harmful to those involved and eventually to society as a whole. Thus, Judaism has effective defensive measures to prevent situations that could lead to uncontrolled lust and wrongful intimacy. For example, there is a concept of *yichud* —

of a man not being alone with a woman who is not his wife. Modesty in dress is an understandable and inseparable part of this pattern of defensive measures.

Much of what passes as acceptable in today's entertainment world is certainly in opposition to Jewish ideas of modesty in speech, dress and behavior. Thus, the tenacity of Jews in retaining the traditional role of modesty in their lives is greatly tested in today's society. Yet, one of the great contributions of Judaism has been to achieve a balance in matters of human sexuality, walking sure-footedly on the tightrope between celibacy and prudishness on one hand and promiscuity and wanton lust on the other hand. That tightrope is anchored by the Jewish concept of modesty in all of its forms.

73 Jewish Hats

nyone observing Orthodox Jewish men at prayer or even on the public street notices that hats, usually black ones, are in style. I am not only referring to *kippot* (also known as *yarmulkes*) that Jews wear as a sign of reverence to the Almighty Who reigns above us, but I am discussing fedoras, fur hat *shreimels*, homburgs, turbans and various other forms of headgear. What is this fixation with hats? Why has a hat — and what type of hat it is — come to identify what kind of Jew the wearer is and with which group in Jewish society he identifies himself?

Hats have a long and distinguished history in Jewish life. The *kippah/yarmulke* is mentioned in the Talmud as a sign of reverence to God and a reminder of the Divine Presence to the wearer. Jewish law mandates keeping one's head covered during prayer, reciting blessings and eating food. Many Orthodox Jews keep their heads covered when walking outside and even at all times within one's home. There are those who wear a "sleep" *yarmulke* when they rest at night. But in Jewish law and Orthodox practice, a *kippah* is not technically a hat.

The Talmud informs us that the Torah scholars wore a special hat — *sudar* — over their *kippah*. Thus, rabbis and deans of Torah schools were always identified by their distinctive hats. These hats naturally varied in appearance from community to community and also from era to era, but Torah scholars wearing hats became a constant in Jewish life. Because of this, the students in the Torah academies, the budding scholars of the future, also wore hats, even though they were not the same style and size as those of their elders and mentors. As a sign of respect for Torah and prayers (and inherently, therefore, for the God of Israel as well) these hats were worn during prayer and on the street. Eventually, Jewish law suggested that during prayer, blessing after meals and other solemn occasions, hats be worn over and above the usual *kippah*.

During the Middle Ages, as part of its campaign of degrading Jews and Judaism, the Catholic Church forced Jews to wear "Jew hats." These hats were usually outlandish in their color and appearance, a form of a dunce cap. The Jewish retaliation for this attempt to humiliate them was to adopt the hat as a badge of pride. Thus, wearing a hat became a Jewish thing, a form of self-identity and an assertion of Judaic faith. Even when this hateful decree finally lapsed, Jews proudly continued to wear their hats. It became ingrained in Ashkenazic Jewish society to wear hats. In the Sephardic world, the social prominence of hats was not as widespread or important as it was among their Ashkenazic brethren. Nevertheless, the Sephardic rabbis and Torah scholars all wore special turbans that identified them as being Jews and Torah scholars.

In the eighteenth century, concurrent with the rise of the Chassidic movement, Polish and Russian noblemen wore fur-trimmed hats as a mark of importance. The great Rebbes of *Chassidut* adopted this form of headgear for their hat for Shabbat, holidays and days of personal joy and significance. The type of fur-trimmed hat — *shtreimel*, *spodek*, etc. — varied from Chassidic court to Chassidic court and from place to place. Because of the expense of this fur-trimmed hat, the masses of Chassidic Jews in Eastern Europe were precluded from wearing this hat. Instead they wore caps, hats and other forms of head-coverings. In today's much more affluent Jewish world, most Chassidim possess a fur-trimmed hat. The exceptions to this rule are the Chabad Chassidim who don black, pinched fedoras, as per their individual tradition and the custom of the last Lubavitcher Rebbe himself.

Jewish dress has always been an adaptation of the dress of the surrounding society in which they lived. Nevertheless, Jews found a way to make that dress represent themselves, their Jewish uniqueness and their role as servants of God and Jewish destiny. Thus, even though Jewish dress has often been scorned and ridiculed, and the wearing of hats in our currently hatless society is questioned and criticized, the significance of observant Jewish garb should never be minimized or dismissed. Distinctive dress helps keep one Jewish in an overwhelmingly non-Jewish world. So, the next time you see a Jew wearing a hat, remember that there is a long and noble story behind it!

74 Respect

The Torah admonishes us to "rise before the elderly and honor the presence of the wise." In the modern world, we are faced with a paradoxical situation. More of us are living longer, becoming older, yet the respectful attitude towards attaining advanced age is becoming quite ambivalent. The marketing of goods in the media is almost always directed at the young or those who pursue the eternal fountain of youth. Retirement homes and senior citizen residences are increasingly popular. But, too often, these places show limited respect or sensitivity to the aging residents.

In the same vein, we pay great lip service to the cause of education, but give very limited respect or concern to the educators. There are many reasons for this, some of which are caused by the teachers and their labor unions themselves, but the culture of our modern world leaves little room for true respect for elders and teachers.

The emphasis in Torah on respect for elders and teachers was reflected in the everyday life and behavior of Jews over the centuries. Even today, in yeshivot (Jewish religious schools) students arise when the teacher enters the room or when the head of the school passes in the study hall. Several centuries ago, it was surmised that this behavior could create an educational problem, for students would be bobbing up and down all day long, distracted from their studies. Tosafot (an in-depth analysis of the Talmud composed by the disciples of the school of Rashi in the twelfth and thirteenth centuries in France and Germany) advances the recommendation that standing for the teachers or the head of the school need occur only once, at the start of each day. In all religious Jewish schools, respect for teachers and elders is a prime value, taught not only in theory but in everyday practice as well.

Respect for teachers is not limited to great scholars and heads of Talmudic academies. It is related that, even later in life, when he achieved widespread fame as a foremost Talmudist and scholar, Rabbi Chaim Soloveitchik of Volozhin and Brisk would rise in honor of the simple teacher who taught him the Hebrew alphabet when he was a child. He was heard to remark: "Everything that man *ever* taught me has remained true my entire life. An *aleph* still is an *aleph* and a *bet* still is a *bet*. Much of what I learned from greater scholars later in my life regarding more complicated scholarship has not stood the test of time and detailed analysis as well as the alphabet I learned from this childhood teacher!" In *Avot* (*Ethics of the Fathers,* one of the 63 volumes of the Mishnah), we are taught that King David lavished grateful praise on a teacher from whom he had learned only two minor halachic matters.

Respect for teachers is based on the Torah principle that we must express our gratitude to those who have helped us in our lives. As such, our teachers who have given us the great gift of knowledge are certainly entitled to our thanks and respect.

There are no perfect teachers, just as there are no perfect parents. If respect for parents, elders and teachers were conditional on their being perfect, then few would earn total respect. The Torah therefore wisely mandates that respect be shown to them, even when one recognizes their human faults and short-comings. I have found in life that people who habitually give respect also command respect from others. Respect for others creates self-respect as well. Training our children to demonstrate respect for their elders and teachers engenders personal restraint, thereby creating a more wholesome, harmonious and peaceful society.

Meditation
and Isolation

U   nlike many other faiths, Judaism does not emphasize solitude, isolation and meditation practices. In
fact, Judaism concentrates strongly on the necessity
of community, social interaction, national identification
and solidarity with all other Jews. A monastic life, celibacy, vows of poverty and a renunciation of this world, its
pleasures, problems and opportunities, are all foreign to
the spirit of the Torah and Jewish existence.

The current promotion of isolated meditation as being
somehow a Jewish form of "spirituality" is only another
example of the confusion of Judaism with other faiths,
fads and importations from other cultures that muddle the
modern Jewish scene. Jewish prayer requires a public
quorum and private prayer, no matter how sincere and
devotional it may be, does not allow for the advanced
level of prayer that is the privilege of public prayer.

Throughout Jewish history, the trend towards monasticism and meditation has been decried. God Himself chas-

tised Elijah the Prophet, who after sojourning alone in the desert for a time apparently was reluctant to return to his task of leading and instructing the Jewish People. The Lord sent him forth on his mission and refused to allow him to wallow in pessimism and self-pity, emotions that prolonged isolation from other humans often breed within us.

The great Rabbi Shimon bar Yochai and his son Elazar spent many years alone in a desert cave, hiding from the Roman authorities who wanted to execute them. When the danger finally passed and the great Rabbi Shimon returned to civilization, he could not bear to see how mundane and even profane life and society were. His years of isolation and meditation made him into a pillar of righteous and holy fire that could no longer abide the seeming pettiness and smallness of everyday human existence. Again, God demanded a change of attitude on the part of the great Rabbi Shimon, lest he be forcibly returned to the isolation of the cave once again and thereby miss the challenge and opportunity for service to Israel that the Lord has envisioned for him.

In later times, the great Chassidic masters often opted for periods of isolation, retreating to the forests for meditation and self-renewal. Yet, this practice also brought upon them criticism from their colleagues and certainly from the masses of Israel who needed a live Rebbe present to tend to them, and not an absent spiritual figure engaged in self and meditation. The great success of the Chassidic movement lay in the closeness and accessibility of the holy leader with the ordinary people who relied on him for guidance, advice, blessing and inspiration.

However, at times, periods of isolation and meditation were recognized as necessary for spiritual leadership to be effective. Thus, it was customary that during the month of Elul, rabbis, Chassidic leaders and other spiritual teachers would absent themselves from their public duties and devote themselves to isolated spiritual meditation and self-analysis. The great men of the Mussar movement practiced these methods of self-introspection daily, albeit for only relatively short periods of daily time. But Elul was always a special time when the barriers against prolonged isolation and personal meditation were relaxed in order to allow one to prepare properly for the Days of Awe and judgment that herald the onset of the Jewish new year.

So, as in everything else, balance becomes the rule of the Torah. Some meditation and isolation, in the proper time and of short duration, is beneficial. Unrestrained mystical behavior and monasticism is not part of the Jewish way of life and Godly holiness.

76 Faith and Miracles

The subject of miracles is one of great importance in Jewish history. The Ten Plagues, the splitting of the Red Sea (literally, the Reed Sea), the heavenly food called manna, the Revelation at Sinai, are all at the foundation of the history of the Jewish People. To Jews, these events are facts of our existence. It signified from our beginnings that we would not have an ordinary history; that to a great extent the Jewish story would be an exception to all of the accepted theories and patterns of human and national existence.

But miracles do not create faith or observance of tradition. They have at most a temporary effect upon those who witness them. The Golden Calf was built and worshipped by people who had witnessed the Ten Plagues in Egypt and had walked over dry land through the Red Sea. The entire forty-year experience of Israel in the Sinai Desert as recorded in the Bible is one of complaints, rebellion, ingratitude and lack of faith. The prophet Elijah brings down miraculous fire from heaven and bests the false prophets of the idol Baal in front of tens of thousands. The Jews all bow down in awe and proclaim that the "God of Israel is the Lord." Nevertheless, they soon revert to their idolatrous behavior and worship. Such is the impact of miracles: They serve a temporary purpose, but do not guarantee loyalty.

Judaism therefore is not built upon miracles, even though miracles form an important part of the Jewish story. The Jewish People are able to identify with the events of the deliverance from Egyptian slavery after thousands of years, not because of the memory of miracles, but rather because of the observance of Passover ritual and custom. It is the actual participation in the Seder, eating the matzoh, abstaining from eating *chametz* (leavened foods) that creates the historical bond that survives all of the generations. Faith is created by ritual and tradition. Miracles are ancillary to that process.

In one of his most famous statements, Maimonides teaches that "miracles" are unable to make what is inherently false true. That is really the crux of the matter. Every religion proclaims its own "miracles." But the Jewish People, perhaps more than those of any other faith, were never swayed in their faith by claimed "miracles." The Jewish People saw itself challenged by the special mission and fate that their experience at Mount Sinai and the God of history placed upon it: to remain strong in faith, to influence all of mankind, to attempt to be a "light unto the nations" and to keep the vision of morality and harmony alive in a very hostile world.

There are a large number of people in Israel that hope for a miraculous deliverance from our present difficulties. I am one of them. But a clear reading of Jewish history indicates that God's hand protects us through events that appear to be natural.

The solution to our problems often lies within ourselves. And that is where inner strength, faith and fortitude play the main role. In fact, it is the ability of the Jewish People to create this inner faith on a constant basis, generation after generation, which is close to being miraculous. But faith requires effort, a traditional way of life and a historical perspective. Let us be worthy of that faith and history.

77 Biblical Heroes

One of the tactics of those who currently deny Jewish uniqueness is to destroy the heroes of the Bible and of Jewish history. This tactic has been employed by many "Biblical scholars" over the past two centuries. It continues today as a weapon among those who somehow believe that there can be a Judaism that is completely disconnected from the Bible, the Talmud, Jewish law and 3,300 years of Jewish tradition.

I believe that the traditional Jewish viewpoint about our Biblical heroes should be presented to the public, unencumbered by the pseudoscience of Biblical criticism and historical revisionism. I have always found it difficult to understand how thousands of years after the fact, people feel they are able to interpret and reach conclusions about the ancients — conclusions that were not evident at that time to contemporaries who knew them, and also escaped the attention of scholars who pored over and continually commented upon the Bible and its heroes over the past many centuries. To me, it smacks of arrogance that a Jewish Studies professor of today should consider himself a greater expert on the Bible and its heroes than, let us say, Rashi or Maimonides.

Jewish tradition treats the heroes of the Bible with great respect, honor and trepidation. Our belief in the divinity and eternity of Torah is directly associated with the belief in the greatness of our teacher Moses. Moses is the "father of all prophets;" the man who spoke with God "fact to face," so to speak; who brought the Torah down from Mount Sinai; who spent forty days on that mountain without food or water and whose presence and leadership forged a group of newly freed slaves into a mighty and influential people. Bluntly put, without Moses and his uniqueness, holiness and supreme gift of prophecy, there is no Torah and hence, no Judaism. Therefore, treating Moses as though he were one of us, a regular guy, with the ordinary faults and virtues of our contemporaries is ignorance, at best, and a direct undermining of Jewish faith and tradition.

The Talmudic view of the matter is succinctly put: "If those who preceded us were to be considered as angels, then we can consider ourselves as human beings. However, if those who preceded us are to be considered as human beings, then we can be considered as only donkeys..."

One of the hallmarks of all the stories in the Bible regarding our great heroes, the patriarchs and matriarchs of Israel, the kings and prophets, the warriors and holy people, is the analytical, critical and unsparing look at their lives and behavior. The Bible presents for us no hagiographic biographies. The Bible teaches us that no human being is perfect and that there is a great deal that we can learn about ourselves and our true nature by studying the lives of the great heroes of our past and taking note of their behavior and their trials in life.

However, just as the Bible phrase "God's anger" cannot be taken literally, (God, by definition, is above any manifestation of human emotion. The phrase is only used to enable humans to somehow deal in our finite way with the Infinite One.) so too, for example, Moses' "anger" and David's "loves" are not to be understood in the same terms as our current-day anger or loves. This pillar of Jewish belief and worldview supports the entire structure of Jewish faith and Judaism's eternal promise.

By destroying our heroes and reducing our past into shameful shabbiness we are drilling a hole in the deck of the ship on which we are sailing. It seems that willingness for self-destruction is unfortunately an ever-present feature of modern Jewish life. Hence, all of the current rage about revising and destroying our heroic past. But modern revisionism will too pass, as have all other attempts to defeat Israel and its Book of Books.

78 Words of Prophecy

Reading the Bible, one will always be struck by the magnificent prose and message of the prophets of Israel. Even translated into all the different languages of mankind, the force, beauty and poignancy of the original Hebrew words of their prophecies come through. Isaiah, Amos, Micah, Jeremiah, Ezekiel and all of their colleagues speak to us today in our difficult situation as though they were being interviewed on today's media. That is the lasting blessing of prophecy. It does not become stale or irrelevant. It is always current, immediate and to the point.

The prophets of Israel, as did the Torah itself, warned the Jewish People against forsaking their beliefs and traditions and worshipping "strange gods." They stated that the Jewish People would suffer greatly if they followed such a wrong path. They also stated that should the people stray, the Lord would nevertheless protect the Jewish People from utter annihilation. He would allow them to survive, bloody but unbowed; but He would also require that they return to Him, to His Torah and to the Jewish way of life.

The prophets preached the necessity of personal honesty, morality and loyalty in both private and public Jewish life. They emphasized the holiness of the Shabbat, the devotion to charitable deeds and of maintaining merciful attitudes. They spoke of the constant need for rededication to the uniqueness of the Jewish People and their mission to spread Godliness and morality in the world. The prophets criticized sexual licentiousness, loose morals, the pursuit of wealth and hedonism. Though they never preached poverty as a virtue, they posed wealth as a challenge. They were fearless in describing the painful consequences of pagan behavior, sexual immorality, and of lives exclusively devoted to revelry.

And all of their words came true in the past and rise to hover over us even now in our present world. The Jewish world is torn today between the prevalent ideas of Western — especially American — culture and society, and its basic roots in the words of its Torah and prophets. The modern world, with all of its glittering advances and its sense of freedom that it has brought to Jews after centuries of persecution, has nevertheless proven to be very unkind to us.

Why do I say unkind? The past century saw over seven million Jews destroyed in the name of all sorts of strange gods. The Jewish family structure has been severely damaged. We are plagued by divorce, a low Jewish birth rate, alienation from the traditions and values of Judaism, and an astounding rate of intermarriage. Even our return to our homeland of Israel is fraught with dangers, peril and doubts. If the prophets of Israel stood before us today, they would not have to revamp their words. All of their ideas, warnings and hopes clearly apply to our current Jewish world and its manifold problems.

Every Shabbat morning in the synagogue, after the Torah reading is concluded, a portion of the Prophets is read publicly. This custom began when a Roman decree forbade the Jews from publicly reading from the Torah itself. The rabbis of the fourth century substituted the reading of a section of the Prophets instead, and somehow the Romans allowed that to continue. Even after the Roman decree was abandoned and the mighty Roman Empire disappeared from the face of the earth, those wise rabbis did not revoke the custom of reading from the Prophets. The timelessness of their messages was such that Jews longed to hear weekly what the prophets of old had to say regarding their current lives and society.

It is no exaggeration to say that the prophets of Israel have accompanied us on our millennia long road over the world landscape. They have also accompanied us back to the Land of Israel and many of their words of hope and achievement have been fulfilled before our very eyes. But they also warned us of the dangers of following strange gods. We would be wise to listen to their words and take their lessons to heart. For they speak the truth about us and about our world.

79 Why We Travel

ews have always been categorized as restless, curious, innovative people. Perhaps it is in our genes, since our father Abraham and mother Sarah were constant travelers. The world is a very interesting place, with a tremendous variety of places and people to see and visit. It is this wondrous variety and fascinating scene that gives testimony to the hand of the Creator in forming our world and the human race. Travel therefore is not only broadening and educational, it can also serve as a basis for faith and inner inspiration. It is perhaps this face of travel that so intrigues Jews and makes us always interested in touring far off places. We are really in search of ourselves when we journey to see others.

Jews are inveterate travelers, continual tourists and always ready to see new places. Part of this may be attributable to our long history of exile and its attendant wanderings. But Jews were travelers even during the time of the First Temple, the height of Jewish national power in the Land of Israel. There were Jewish colonies in Greece and Ethiopia during the reign of King Solomon. The original cause for such Jewish journeys was undoubtedly commercial. But Jews settled permanently in many parts of the Mediterranean basin and soon began journeying eastward towards Persia and India. Again, the reasons for these migrations were primarily commercial ones.

It is difficult for us in the twenty-first century to imagine what the conditions of travel were like for our ancestors. Suffice it to say that the travel that we now measure in hours and achieve in relative comfort (though there are economy coach seats on some airplanes that are a throwback to past travel hardships) were then measured in months and entailed great danger to property and life. In the thirteenth century, the great Jewish traveler, Benjamin of Tudela, left Spain for a tour of the Jewish world that lasted for years. He left us a recorded journal of his travels and visits, his impressions of the Jewish communities and their leaders and a fascinating description of life in the Middle Ages in the Mediterranean basin and beyond. It is interesting to note that on all of his journeys he always met other Jews who were also traveling. This at a time when the vast majority of the world's population never strayed more than twenty-five kilometers from their hometown during their entire life span.

Jews were forced to migrate because of expulsions, persecution and pogroms. The Jews were expelled from England and France in the high Middle Ages and from Spain at the end of the fifteenth century. Pogroms and violent Christian enmity forced the Jews of Central Europe to move eastward to Poland and Lithuania in the fourteenth century. The Jews were of necessity a mobile people, always searching for a safe haven and a decent place to settle and live as Jews.

In the eighteenth century, another inveterate traveler, Rabbi Chaim Yosef David Azulai — known as "Chida" — journeyed throughout the Jewish world as a latter-day Benjamin of Tudela. Chida's purpose was to collect funds for the support of the small Jewish community in Jerusalem that he represented. A dedicated scholar and a person of great curiosity and investigative skills, he spent more time in libraries and bookshops than collecting money for his cause. His letters and writings provide us with an insight into Jewish life in Europe and the Mediterranean basin at the dawn of the modern era of world history. Thus his writings more than compensate for his apparently meager fundraising abilities.

The narratives of Jewish travelers, like those of Benjamin of Tudela, are often replete with references to the Jews in other lands. As a matter of course, traveling Jews always connected with fellow Jews in the countries they visited, both for protection as well as fellowship. They were in need of kosher food, prayer services and an understanding companion. Their observance of Torah law and their common goals (as well as their usual knowledge of Hebrew as a Jewish universal language) united them in global brotherhood. Today many Jews continue to follow this precedent, seeking out the Jewish communities in their travel destinations. There is nothing like walking into a synagogue in Hoboken or Hong Kong and noting that no matter what the cultural differences, Jews are in reality merely a far-flung family, eager to share their hospitality with others.

80 Music

s in many other fields of human endeavor and talent, Jews have been disproportionately represented in the field of music. Heifetz, Horowitz, Rubenstein, Perlman, Stern, Gershwin, Kern, Mahler and Bernstein are all remembered as being part of a long list of master performers, conductors and composers of the past century who were Jewish. The connection of Jews to music is deep and traditional. Originally, it was always nurtured in a framework of liturgy, prayer and Sabbath and holiday joy. However, when the world became more open to Jews in the nineteenth and twentieth centuries, Jews entered into all of the fields of music — religious, classical, popular, opera and the musical stage. Many of these virtuosos were former cantors, such as Al Jolson, Richard Tucker and Jan Peerce. Their Jewish experience was somehow reflected in their performances on the concert and operatic stage.

Thousands of years ago, the daily service of the Temple in Jerusalem included a musical performance by the Levites.

These performances were famous worldwide and, according to Josephus, hundreds of thousands of non-Jewish visitors came to Jerusalem to hear the famous orchestra and choir of the Levites.

Psalm 137 records the request of the Babylonian conquerors of Jerusalem that the Levites perform for them in concert in Babylonia. The woeful answer of the Levites was, "How could we sing the song of the Lord on foreign soil?" Tradition tells us that the Levite harpists purposely maimed their thumbs so that they would be physically unable to perform the Temple music for their Babylonian captors. They hung their harps on the willow trees "by the rivers of Babylon" and lamented the tragedy of the destruction of the Temple and the Jewish state. A new melody, a dirge of lamentation, was created in the Jewish world to accompany the reading of Jeremiah's Book of Lamentations/*Eichah* on the ninth day of the Jewish month of Av, the anniversary of the fall of Jerusalem.

After the destruction of the Second Temple by the Romans in the year 70 CE, the desolation among Jews was so great that almost all forms of music were eliminated from Jewish public life. Even today, many Jews in Jerusalem allow only one musical instrument, besides a drum, to be played at weddings and other festive occasions.

Jewish musical talent was therefore confined to the synagogue and the liturgy of prayer. Great Jewish musicians became cantors in the synagogue or composers of liturgical pieces. Later, in the late Middle Ages, roving bands of Jewish musicians — called in *Yiddish, klezmer*, a contraction of the two Hebrew words *klei zemer* (musical instruments of song) — performed at weddings, dedications of a Torah scroll and other festive occasions.

Traditional melodies for Sabbath songs, holiday liturgy and especially music for the High Holy Days, developed in all Jewish communities. These melodies reflected the surrounding cultures where Jews lived, with the Sephardic Jews mirroring the influence of Oriental and Arabic music in their melodies while their Ashkenazic brethren introduced German and Slavic overtones to their traditional liturgical melodies.

In the twentieth century, Israeli music, as well as takeoffs on Eastern European Chassidic music, became popular in the Jewish world, both within the confines of the synagogue and outside of it. Such balladeers as Shlomo Carlebach, Mordechai ben David, Avraham Fried and others became concert performers and their melodies were even adopted and adapted in the synagogue services. Large Jewish orchestral groups regularly perform at concerts and weddings. Even the styles of modern music — rock, jazz, country — and other forms of current popular music were incorporated within the broad category of "Jewish music."

Music is a soulful experience, one that touches emotion and sentiment. Its many expressions reflect the soul of our People, which is why it is continually changing and popular.

81 The Arts

Because of the Torah prohibition, recorded in the Ten Commandments, forbidding the creation of human, animal or astronomical forms of idols, Jews did not engage in the type of arts that were common in the ancient world. Since statues, paintings and decorations were used in pagan worship services, the arts were never seen as part of Jewish life in those times. When the Greeks insisted on erecting a statue of Zeus in the Temple of Jerusalem, the Jews reacted in horror and rebellion. Nevertheless, as the Greeks and Romans began to disassociate their art forms from their own already waning beliefs in paganism, the revulsion of the Jews to the works of art also began to diminish.

The earliest Jewish art of which we have a record, outside of the great artifacts of the Temple in Jerusalem, are mosaic floors of synagogues that date back to the fifth century and were very popular during the entire early Byzantine Christian period. Such floors are found in many locations in Israel and in other areas of the Middle East.

With the rise of Christian art in the Middle Ages, especially the use of stained glass, Jewish buildings began to reflect this growing trend. Though Jews did not match the color and intensity (and certainly not the themes) of Christian stained glass, we do see colored windows in synagogues in the fourteenth century. During the Middle Ages, Jewish art was reflected in the illuminations that decorated Jewish prayer books, Bibles and other works of scholarship. Though much of the artwork in these manuscripts and books was done by non-Jews, Jewish artists began to emerge then as well.

It was during the Renaissance period that Jews began to dabble notably in the arts, especially in painting. The Jews in Holland in the sixteenth and seventeenth centuries were great patrons of the arts, if not artists themselves. Rembrandt painted many Jewish subjects and many Jews were his patrons and customers. There are a number of paintings of the great Spanish-Portuguese Synagogue in Amsterdam hanging in the world's famous art museums, as well as portraits of some of the great rabbis of the city such as Jacob Sassportas and Zvi Ashkenazi. However, the synagogues themselves in Amsterdam were devoid of any art or stained glass and their beauty lay in the magnificent mahogany panels that formed the wall of the Torah Ark.

In Poland, beginning in the seventeenth century, there were synagogues that were decorated with paintings. Tapestries that covered the ark and the Torah scrolls contained two-dimensional figures of lions, birds and other figures. All of this caused rabbinical discussion regarding the propriety of such art in the synagogue, but in a short period of time such displays of art became acceptable in synagogues throughout the world.

Jewish art over most of the last thousand years was concentrated on the creation of Judaica. Jewish ritual artifacts such as etrog containers, candlesticks, wine cups, Torah ornaments and crowns, Chanukah lamps and Purim accessories, were all outlets for the talents of Jewish artisans and smiths. In the modern era, many Jewish painters achieved fame, if not necessarily fortune. Some of them, such as Chagall and Raskin, portrayed Jewish subjects, while others, such as Pissaro, painted only general themes. Still later in our times, many Israeli painters achieved notice and recognition.

Jewish homes also began to display paintings as part of their decor. Most traditional homes today have paintings or pictures of great rabbis or holy places in Israel on the walls of their homes. The use of stained glass windows in synagogues is widespread. Art, like all other human endeavors, can be sanctified or cheapened. Jewish art, therefore, should reflect values and norms consistent with our holy Torah and the high moral values it is our mission to teach the world.

82 Sports

We are all aware that sports is a multi-billion dollar industry with enormous effect and influence upon its millions of followers. The thrills, excitement and pleasure that sports provides for its followers is immeasurable, even though the high costs of being a spectator to the events of sports is painfully calculable. The devotion of fans to their favorite teams borders upon idol worship and has many times spilled over into violence. The modern world is hooked on sports.

The Jewish attitude regarding sports is a different one than that of most of the world. Judaism encourages athletic exercise, care of the body, activity, ingenuity, physical strength and well-being. It does not encourage violent behavior of one human being against another. Thus boxing, wrestling, judo, violent contact sports such as ice hockey, rugby and tackle football, would seem to fall outside the acceptable pale of permitted sports. Yet, we find in the rabbinic writings of the early Middle Ages that Jews engaged in jousting tournaments to enliven weddings and "gladden the bride and groom!" The rabbis seemed to oppose the practice, but who listens to rabbis?

One of the strongest objections that the Jews had to the Greek and Roman culture in their midst was to their sporting activities. The mandatory nudity of the participants; the accompanying drunken spectacles; sexual orgies and animal sacrifices to the pagan gods (which were part and parcel of the sporting events) also were condemned by most Jews. The use of gladiators — sports events that were predetermined to cost human lives — sickened the Jews, who believe that human life is the highest value in society. Making a sport out of maiming or killing someone was and is repugnant to the ethos of traditional Judaism.

The ancient sports arena glorified, even deified, man and the body over spiritual and intellectual attainments. In a pagan society, man could become a god, as did Hercules and other physically powerful figures. These ideas were anathema to the Jews, for whom the line between man and God was clearly and irrevocably drawn. For Jews, man's physical prowess was recognized as fleeting, while one's spiritual attainments remained eternal.

The current rampant and outlandish commercialization of sports, the exploitation of the athletes (no matter how high their salaries are) and the attendant hoopla of questionable good taste and borderline behavior that invariably accompany sporting events also are foreign to the Jewish spirit and noble view of human behavior.

In the mid-twentieth century, Jews looked at organized sports in a different light. Jewish sportsmen, fans, team owners, sports writers, media broadcasters and commentators abounded. It was as though the Jews became sports crazed, since this avenue of activity served as their confirmation of being fully accepted into modern society. It was Hank Greenberg and Sandy Koufax who blazed the path of success for Jewish American acceptability, long before Jewish CEO's of major American corporations became more common. Thus, many Jews became and are inveterate sports fans (and even team owners), not only for the love of the game itself, but also for the unseen yet essential benefit of societal acceptability that the sports arena ostensibly affords them.

In Israel, the same benefit of international acceptance and respectability fueled the development of Israel's sports leagues and teams. The appearance of Israel at the Olympics has become a matter of national self-vindication. How else can we explain the muted Israeli reaction to the murder of its athletes at the Olympic Games in Germany, or the refusal of the UEFA Soccer League to play its games in Tel Aviv? Would not a proud nation disdain participation in international sports events so politically biased and insensitive to its people? But it is the drive that we must somehow belong — and participation in sports means belonging — that fuels Israel's desire to participate at all costs, no matter what the price or the shame.

I am not writing this as a killjoy or in opposition to organized sports. I definitely appreciate the beauty of a well-turned double play or a fabulous three-point shot at the buzzer. I merely raise the issue that sports, like all other areas of modern life, should be seen within the wide and deep perspective of Jewish tradition. As such, we will be able to absorb the good, enjoy the game and discard the large amount of chaff that abounds in today's sporting society.

83 Ecology

The Bible teaches us that humans were given the right to rule over the planet Earth for their benefit. We are entitled to mine its riches, use its animals, birds, fish and other organisms for our sustenance and health. And we are awestruck and inspired by the beauty and complexity of its nature. Nowhere, however, was mankind given the right to destroy or even injure the world that was given it for its use. The Torah specifically forbids wanton destruction of trees and the rabbis extended that injunction to all other forms of natural resources of this earth. There is a prohibition against waste and destruction — *baal tashchit,* "do not destroy" — that is the basis for the Jewish attitude toward every animate and even inanimate object in our world.

This prohibition of *baal tashchit* is mentioned in the Torah as operative even in regard to wartime conditions, when nations usually mobilize and exploit all resources in order to achieve victory. How much more so is it applicable to our ordinary, everyday lives. The Jewish position on ecology is part of a wider attitude against wasting anything. Frugality, though not miserliness, has always been a virtue touted by our tradition. Benjamin Franklin's adage of "waste not, want not," certainly coincides with Jewish thinking and values. Thus "waste not" refers to the natural resources and scenic treasures of our planet. The Jewish attitude on ecology is also heavily influenced by the reverence for life that is the basis of all Jewish ethics.

Legend has it that the great Rabbi Abraham Kook, the first chief rabbi of what was then Palestine, reprimanded one of his disciples for absentmindedly tearing a leaf off a tree branch. "You should let living things continue to live," he said. Certainly, wanton destruction of animal and plant life and habitat is clearly in opposition to Torah standards and values.

Yet an important caveat must be added to this discussion on ecology. In Jewish thought, all ecological rights and privileges must be measured and balanced in the light of continuing human needs and civilization's progress. The enthusiasm of environmentalists sometimes makes their proposals unbalanced and unrealistic. The Torah recognizes the supremacy of man in this world and mankind therefore has the right to utilize, but again not to unalterably destroy, the natural resources that the earth has provided for the technological advancement of the human condition.

As I have mentioned so often in this book, Judaism is a religion of balance and realism. Thus the attitude of saving our natural habitat and avoiding any violation of the *baal tashchit* principle must be balanced with the needs and benefits of humans. There are no clear lines in reaching such a decision, for the needs of mankind and the circumstances of world ecology are always changing. But again, as in all other areas of life, the unchanging principles of the Torah that should govern our decisions are clear.

The Torah demanded that we leave for our children and their descendants a fruitful, productive and beautiful world. This can only be accomplished if we are truly aware of the ecological problems that confront us and take steps to safeguard this sacred trust of our beautiful natural world for later generations. Judaism ordains blessings to be recited when witnessing the wonders of nature — mountains, seas and scenes of grandeur. The recitation of these blessings impress upon us that all of the world, with its intricately balanced chain of food and life, testifies to the handiwork of the Creator Who has fashioned such a wondrous earth for us to live upon.

84 Animal Rights

O ver the past few decades, animal rights activists have been very active in opposing the use of animals in medical experiments and research on human diseases. They have also been opposed to the human use of leather, meat and fur. Sometimes their means of opposition has been extreme and even violent, so convinced are they of the moral justice of their cause.

The truth is that according to Jewish law and tradition, animals do have rights. But like all moral rights, these have to be judged in perspective, balanced with other moral rights and with proper standards. The Torah itself provides certain basic standards in regard to animal rights and the use of animals generally by humans for their own personal gain and purposes. Here are a few examples of the Torah's attitude on the treatment of animals by humans.

We read in the Bible about the prohibition of overloading a beast of burden. If one sees such an animal being crushed under the weight that it is forced to carry, one must assist in unloading the burden from that animal. This is true even if the owner of that animal is personally unworthy of your help in the matter. The animal is not to be made to suffer because of the bad behavior of its owner.

The Torah teaches us that one is obligated to feed one's animals before being allowed to sit down to eat his own meal. Reverence for life is such an integral part of Judaism that unnecessary killing of harmless insects and other creatures is unacceptable. Even animals destined to be slaughtered for their meat are to be treated with kindness. The Talmud tells us that the great Rabbi Yehuda HaNasi, the editor of the Mishnah and the leader of second century Jewry, was punished by Heaven for his lack of compassion for a calf being led to slaughter. Mankind may use animals for its benefit. It is not allowed to wantonly abuse animal life for sport, pleasure or malice.

One of the cardinal principles of the Torah is the avoidance of *tzar baalei chayim* — causing pain to living creatures. Wanton destruction of animal life is forbidden. In a famous responsa (rabbinical reply to a legal question), the eighteenth century scholar and rabbi of Prague, Rabbi Yechezkel Landau, forbids hunting animals or birds for sport.

What about the slaughtering of animals for food? Even in the slaughterhouse, the Jewish method of *shechitah* — slitting the animal's throat with a surgically sharp knife that has no imperfections in its blade — is much less painful than other forms of slaughtering animals. The animal is usually dead within six seconds.

Mankind may use animals to further human comfort, work and health and to create a better society. The Torah states that this privilege to use animals for human benefit was granted to mankind by God Himself. Without rhesus monkeys there would have been no polio vaccine. Artificial limbs, organ transplants, miracle drugs and revolutionary surgical procedures all have been a fabulous boon to mankind, especially over the past decades of breathtaking medical progress.

In God's world, animal rights are relative and not absolute, secondary to human progress and health. Animal species are not to be made extinct in order to produce exotic purses, but the use of animals to save and improve human lives is essential and permissible. It is part of man's pact with nature and its Creator. Those who place animal life over human life were judged negatively by the prophets of Israel, and the principle stands to this day: "Those who kiss calves are those who slaughter humans," i.e. those who place animal rights over human life and the progress of civilization have misplaced, unbalanced values. The Torah demands perspective in our behavior. That perspective and balance is necessary in man's relationship with the animal world as well.

85 Bigotry and Hatred

The incidence of anthrax terrorism in the United States created great panic in the population. Even though the number of actual anthrax cases was relatively minute when compared to the size of the population, the panic was great and all-pervasive. Even more than bombs and explosions — which are, after all, at least visible forms of violence and death — plague and disease are more fearsome and sow unreasonable panic among a civilian population precisely because they are unseen and their true causes unknown. The difficulties encountered by the American law enforcement agencies in identifying the source of the anthrax plague only intensified the feeling of fear and helplessness in the general American population.

In the Middle East, the word on the Arab street is that the Jews are the ones who caused the anthrax plague. Since a large section of the Moslem world, if polls are to be believed, is of the opinion that the September 11

Twin Towers tragedy was also of Israeli origin, it is not difficult to realize how they can also believe that the anthrax plague is a Jewish plot.

The Jewish People has had a long and sad history of somehow being held responsible for plagues and disease. During the Middle Ages, when the great bubonic plague epidemic decimated Europe in the fourteenth century, the Jews were accused of poisoning the wells and causing the plague to spread. No logic or reasoning aided the Jewish cause in refuting this fatuous lie. Tens of thousands of Jews throughout Europe were killed by local Christian populations in retaliation for the Jews' "crime" of causing the plague. And even though history, science and common sense (which is unfortunately not very common) have long proven that the Jews had nothing to do with the spread of bubonic plague in Europe at any time in history, the image of the Jew as the spreader of disease remained firmly implanted in the minds of the European non-Jewish population.

Hitler's propaganda machine in the 1930's blamed the unexplainable incidence of polio in German society on the Jews. Jews were always portrayed in Nazi propaganda as bacillus, the carrier of painful diseases meant to destroy non-Jewish society. The neo-Nazi thugs that still abound in the Western world today keep the polio myth alive. They even prove their point by pointing to the fact that the two doctors who eradicated polio through the discovery of vaccines — Jonas Salk and Leonard Sabin — were both Jews. Thus they claimed that the Jews knew how to eradicate polio since they were the ones who created the disease in the first place! This poisonous type of Jew hatred, a plague of major proportions in its own right, has spread to the Moslem Middle East, where Israel and the Jews are generally held responsible for all of the ills of the world.

Thus the bubonic plague calumny was revived in the recent anthrax plague scare in the United States. It is terribly depressing to realize that the lies and evils of the fourteenth century are still current and popularly believed at the dawn of the twenty-first century.

As the Jewish People can well attest, perhaps the worst plague that can afflict and affect mankind is the plague of bigotry and unreasoning hatred. The war against the anthrax-spreaders in our society — whoever they may be — is only indicative of the greater war that must be fought in order to create a safer, saner world society. This greater war is against scapegoating others for one's troubles and problems, of hating others because they are different in appearance and/or faith, of justifying evil and violence in the name of a proclaimed holy cause. This great plague is within our power to control and subdue. No effort should be spared to achieve its permanent cure.

86 Tempered Joy

During the holiday of Passover, the joyous prayer of *Hallel* is recited, as it is on all holidays of the year except for the solemn days of Rosh Hashanah and Yom Kippur. On Purim, the reading of the Book of Esther itself is considered a form of *Hallel*. The *Hallel* comes in two forms — full *Hallel* and an abbreviated form that omits two of its paragraphs. This latter form is called half *Hallel,* though in reality it is 80% of the prayer. On Shavuot, Succot, Shmini Atzeret, Chanukah and the first days of Passover, the full *Hallel* is recited. On Rosh Chodesh (the beginning of each Jewish month) and the final six days of Passover, only the half *Hallel* is recited. The reason for only half *Hallel* on Rosh Chodesh is fairly simple. Rosh Chodesh is, after all, not a holiday and according to Maimonides and other halachic decisors, the recitation of *Hallel* on Rosh Chodesh is based on custom, not on law.

But why do we say the two different versions of *Hallel* on Passover? Why is only the abbreviated form used on the latter days of the holiday? The matter is discussed at length in the works of the rabbis and scholars. I wish to concentrate on one view that is particularly emphasized by Rabbi Meir Simchah HaKohen, the rabbi of Dvinsk, Latvia, eighty years ago.

The seventh day of Passover is the anniversary of the crossing of the Red Sea by the Israelites and the drowning of the Egyptian army that pursued them into the water. Many Egyptians lost their lives on that day. Jews do not celebrate the loss of human life, even of those who were evil and were our oppressors. We celebrate our deliverance and escape from mortal danger, but our joy is tempered — we say half *Hallel* — due to the loss of Egyptian life. We would have preferred to have been left alone to travel out of Egypt and not pursued by Egyptians who wished to kill us. We would have recited full *Hallel* on a bloodless escape from the Egyptians, but that was not to be. It is true that we saw our relentless enemies drown, but any unrestrained exultation on our part is out of place.

The same thought applies to our celebration of Chanukah. The rabbis placed the emphasis of the holiday on the miraculous pitcher of oil and the light of the Menorah in the Temple. There is no special celebration of the military victories of the Hasmoneans and no mementos of the terrible and bloody defeats inflicted on the Syrian Greeks. We celebrate our deliverance and independence, but take very little relish in the necessity of having to kill thousands of our enemies in order to obtain our deliverance. Therefore, the centerpiece of the holiday is the Menorah and the oil and not the terrible war that preceded it.

The same idea is reflected in the holiday of Purim. The celebration of the date of the holiday is on the fourteenth and fifteenth days of the Hebrew month of Adar, but not on the thirteenth of Adar. This date is the actual date of the war of self-defense that the Jews fought against their enemies. It resulted in thousands of their persecutors being killed. The celebration is on the fourteenth and fifteenth days of Adar — the days that the Jews felt free and saved from danger, but not on the day of the killing itself.

King David, who was the righteous king of Israel and saved the Jewish People from its centuries-old, relentless enemies such as the Philistines and Amalekites, was not permitted by God to build the First Holy Temple. The Temple was not to be built by a warrior, no matter how necessary and justified his battles. His son, King Solomon, whose name itself represents peace, fought no wars during his reign. It was he who built the First Temple in Jerusalem.

Obviously, this theme — first taught to us by the laws of *Hallel* — runs throughout our history, and we would do well to dwell on its ramifications even today.

87 The Temple Mount

The public debate about the most contentious issue of sovereignty over the Temple Mount in Jerusalem begs for some historical clarity. Unfortunately, the political posturing and inflammatory rhetoric of the Arabs and the weak public relations effort of the Israelis have only further beclouded the matter. There is an element of spite in all of the discussions regarding the Temple Mount. In the words of the false mother standing before King Solomon and advocating the division of the still living child, "If I can't have it, then neither shall you have it." It is this element of spite, of somehow refusing to cede what is historically correct and proper, that places the solution to the Temple Mount sovereignty problem beyond our current reach.

The Temple Mount is the center of the world according to Jewish tradition. The *Midrash* teaches us that the earth and dust from which original man — Adam — was created was taken from the soil of the Temple Mount. The Temple Mount is named Mount Moriah in the Bible.

Again, according to the *Midrash*, Cain and Abel disputed sovereignty over that holy spot. The Mount therefore was a cause of the first murder in human history. It has unfortunately been the cause of many more since, even till this very day. It was the place that Abraham "saw from afar" when he led Isaac to be sacrificed. It was the place where God instructed him not to harm Isaac and forbade any thought of human sacrifice to Him. Jacob passed and prayed there on his journey into exile to Laban's house. From the beginning of time and recorded history it has been *the place* as far as Judaism is concerned.

The Talmud teaches us that there are three places in the Land of Israel over which there should be no contention as to the Jewish right of sovereignty. They are the Tomb of the Patriarchs in Hebron, Joseph's Tomb near Nablus and the Temple Mount. To all three, the Talmud states that the Jews have a legitimate bill of sale for the properties, since they were purchased in good faith at full price: the sales are recorded in the Bible and have never been challenged. It is therefore doubly ironic that it is these three places that are the most contentious and unfortunately bloody places in today's Jewish-Arab dispute.

It has been pointed out that most Orthodox Jews do not walk on the Temple Mount today. Somehow this has been portrayed as a forfeiture of the Jewish claims of ownership. However, Jews do not refrain from praying on the Mount because it is not ours; we do not pray there precisely because it *is* ours and the special holiness of the Holy Temples' area requires a degree of spiritual purification that we are currently incapable of attaining. Our abstaining from praying there is our strongest act of claiming sovereignty to the mountain. For since the Temple was ours legally, spiritually and historically, the holiness of the place of the Temple remains permanent and subject to the rules of Torah and Jewish law.

There is a prayer that Jews recite during the *Hoshannah* prayers of Succot that contains an alphabetical acrostic of twenty-two names in Biblical and Jewish tradition ascribed to the Temple Mount. One of those twenty-two descriptive names is "*ratzuf ahavah.*" Literally, this name means paved or lined with love. In my opinion, there is no better phrase to describe the relationship of the Jewish People throughout the ages to the Temple Mount than this name. The love and longing, tears and yearning that Jews have invested in this place for thousands of years have alone been a sufficient purchase price to warrant our sovereignty over that holy mountain. We will not prevent the Moslems from praying in the mosques that they erected on the Mount. But the Mount itself belongs to the Jewish People, to its history and to its destiny.

The Greatest
Anti-Semitic Myth

ne of the acts of the original Passover in Egypt was the Jews' placing of the blood of the paschal lamb on the lintel and the doorposts of their homes. When God came to slay the Egyptian firstborns, He "passed over" the Jewish homes that were marked by this symbol of the lamb's blood and the plague was averted therein. The sign of the blood on the doorposts and lintel of the home was the symbol of Jewish faith and loyalty to the God of Israel and to Moses, their leader and savior. Thus was blood — animal's blood — part of the Passover tradition of Israel from the first Passover onwards.

However, later in Jewish history, the connection between blood and Passover became much more sinister. Christianity dealt with blood in a religious and mysterious fashion. Part of Catholic belief came to be that the wine of the Mass was itself a transubstantiation of the blood of Jesus. This belief made a connection between wine and blood. As part of this theological background, to which Jews were the exclusive and very vociferous deniers in Christian Europe in the Middle Ages, the notorious "blood libel" against Jews appeared. This libel, by now already a millennia old, posited that Jews somehow required Christian blood to be mixed into the dough used to bake matzot for Passover, especially for matzot to be eaten at the Seder. This preposterous claim found willing echoes in Christian theological anti-Semitism. The "blood libel" sank deep roots into Christian European society.

Jews actually dreaded the coming of the Passover season because of the anti-Semitism and violence that often accompanied its appearance. There always seemed to be some Christian child that was "lost" during this season and the Jews were accused of kidnapping and killing the child in order to extract Christian blood for the baking of the Passover matzot. No amount of Jewish denial or rational Christian thought could counteract the general belief that the "blood libel" engendered in the general Christian population. No country in Europe that contained a Jewish population was spared the ravages of the "blood libel." And the non-existent incident that sparked a fantastic, unbelievable nightmare of the necessity of Christian blood for Passover many times resulted in the Passover slaughter of thousands of innocent Jews to allegedly revenge a crime that had no basis in fact or reality. Due to this, Jews often used white wine for the Seder instead of red wine, for the stains of the red wine could be misconstrued as being bloodstains.

In 1840, a Christian child disappeared in Damascus, Syria, in the month before Passover. A Catholic priest falsely accused the Jewish community of killing the child for his blood. The leaders of the Jewish community were arrested and under horrific torture "admitted" to their complicity in the "crime." But the accusation of the "blood libel" was so patently false that outside diplomatic pressure was brought on the Sultan of Turkey, then the ruler of Damascus, to free the accused Jews. Sir Moses Montefiore was especially active in saving the lives of the Jews of Damascus, and Queen Victoria provided the necessary diplomatic muscle to enable Montefiore's efforts to be successful. But the "blood libel" did not die so easily.

In the early 1920's, there was a "blood libel" against the Jews living in Messina, New York! The missing child was found before Passover, but the threat of a violent pogrom hung over the Jews of that small upstate New York town. Hitler revived the "blood libel" in its full intensity with his vicious propaganda machine. The belief that Christian blood is needed for Jewish matzoh still exists in certain elements of European society today.

The Arab world, which adopted Hitler's anti-Semitism whole cloth, even now proclaims in its mass media that non-Jewish blood (they say that Muslim blood will also do) is necessary for matzoh baking for Passover.

Lies, at least as far as they pertain to Jews, die hard. Yet each year, false accusations against Israel and the Jews disappear from our minds, and, as we have for centuries, we commence with preparations and share the joy of Passover!

Being Jewish in a Non-Jewish World

he wonder of Jewish history is that the Jewish People survived as an entity in a world of hostility, persecution and discrimination. Being Jewish in a non-Jewish world posed an enormous challenge for the individual Jew and certainly for the People as a whole. There were different challenges to Jewish survival — physical and spiritual — in different times and places. The attempt to answer the challenge of remaining Jewish in a non-Jewish society is really the basis of all events in Jewish history.

Let me share with you an insight of Rabbi Samson Raphael Hirsch in his commentary to the Bible. Rabbi Hirsch was the head of the famous separatist-Orthodox community in Frankfurt-am-Main, Germany, and was the main spokesman and idealogue of the *"Torah im Derech Eretz"* movement. This movement advocated a completely observant Orthodox Jew who was nevertheless imbued with Western culture, university knowledge and degrees, and lived as an integral part of the general

German society that surrounded him. Hirsch believed that this *"Torah im Derech Eretz"* program and outlook was the ultimate solution to the problem of nineteenth century Western European Jewry: How to remain devoutly Jewish after the Enlightenment and Emancipation had destroyed the ghetto walls and ended Jewish isolation in society.

Hirsch observed that there were three levels of Jewish status in the Exile. ("The Exile" refers to the global scattering of the Jewish nation after the destruction of the Second Holy Temple in Jerusalem and the end of Jewish habitation in the Holy Land.) The first is analogous to the status of our father Abraham. "You are a prince of God in our midst," acknowledged the idolatrous society surrounding Abraham. He was free from jealousy and persecution, discrimination or harm. The world respected and honored Abraham and had a deep appreciation towards him for his continuing contributions towards the betterment of society. As such, Abraham's place in general society was secure. Not only was his Jewishness not a liability to him, it was his strongest asset in gaining the respect of the surrounding pagan world.

The second type of status was that of Abraham's son, Isaac. He also had a great influence on others and was able to live a truly Jewish life in an otherwise pagan society. But Isaac was subject to jealousy, verbal and economic harassment and blatant bigotry against him from his non-Jewish neighbors and rulers. Yet, Isaac remained prosperous, strong, faithful and successful. He was not afraid to stand up for his rights to the authorities of government, but he maintained a lower profile than did his father, Abraham.

The third status is that of Jacob. Jacob suffered open persecution, physical threats to his life and worked as a despised serf in a jealous, hostile and always potentially violent non-Jewish society. Jacob was long-suffering, obsequious, yet persistent and stubborn. Nevertheless, he felt himself unable to change his status. His ultimate weapon was his Jewish tenacity and faith. He remained Jewish in spite of the hatred and persecution that surrounded him. Ironically, hatred and persecution always forced Jews to define themselves to themselves, and for most Jews, this process strengthened their Jewish connection.

Hirsch, in the middle of nineteenth century Western European society, claimed that the Jew had risen from the status of Jacob (the Middle Ages) to the status of Isaac (The Enlightenment). Ironically, he speculated that the day would come when the German Jew would attain the status of Abraham. Sadly, he was very wrong in this assessment, for twentieth century Germany would not tolerate the existence of Jewish life whatsoever in its midst, not even in the status of Jacob.

In our current Jewish world, at the beginning of the twenty-first century, we are most tempted to once again say that we have attained the level of Isaac, if not even closer to that of Abraham, in Western society. Only time will tell if this upward trend is real and permanent or, God forbid, only another mirage in our long trek through the desert of history. In any event, the challenge of remaining Jewish in a non-Jewish world — now a new world of technology, instant communication and swirling ideas — remains before us. We must be equal to the test as all past generations of Jews have been, in order to guarantee our survival and to fulfill our God-given mission.

90 **Israel**

J udaism posits that holiness exists in differing degrees in humans, in time and in geographical locations. Much of this book has been devoted to explaining the traditions of the Jewish People regarding human holiness and sanctified behavior. The subject of holiness in time has been discussed as the basis for understanding the Jewish Sabbath and holidays of the year. The holiness of geographical location is focused on the Land of Israel.

Though the Lord is omnipresent in the world and as the great Rebbe of Kotzk, Poland once said, "He can be found wherever one allows Him to enter," the Bible nevertheless describes Israel as the place where "the eyes of the Lord your God are concentrated...[i.e. a concentration of holiness] from the beginning of the year until the end of the year." It is the piece of land that God promised to Abraham, Isaac and Jacob, and to their descendants, the Jewish People. It was the goal of Moses and the Israelites to reach it after forty years of wandering in the desert. And indeed, the Land of Israel was home to the Jewish People for more than 800 years thereafter.

During the long exile of the Jews, as a People dispersed throughout the world for millennia, they never forsook their rights and longing regarding the Land of Israel as their homeland. Jews always pray facing in the direction of Jerusalem. The ardent hope, "Next year in rebuilt Jerusalem" is voiced at the Seder table and at the conclusion of the Yom Kippur services.

It is a little-known fact that there was constant Jewish immigration to Israel throughout the ages, albeit for most generations it was in very small numbers. Even Jews who were or are comfortably and loyally part of other nation states throughout the world always retained a special affection and attachment regarding the Land of Israel.

Beginning in the nineteenth century and throughout the twentieth century, great numbers of Jews immigrated to Israel. Many did so for ideological and religious reasons. For others, the Zionist movement served as a catalyst for their migration from the Diaspora to Israel. However, many non-Zionist Jews also immigrated to Israel, especially for reasons of religious fulfillment and growth.

Hundreds of thousands of Jews immigrated to Israel to escape persecution in the Moslem world, to abandon the blood drenched soil of anti-Semitic Europe and to breathe free after many decades of Communist oppression. This polyglot of people has together formed the new State of Israel.

Israel is the only "comeback" nation in human history. The ancient and medieval empires have all disappeared, as have much of their cultures and languages, but the Jewish People have returned to their ancient homeland in their millions, speaking their ancient and holy original language of Hebrew. Against enormous odds, Jews have built a vibrant, strong, democratic, Jewish society. I think that the State of Israel qualifies as one of the wonders of human history.

It is very difficult to transform a dream into hard reality. The difficult mundane facts of everyday life always jar our hopes and cherished aspirations. The Land of Israel, for most of Jewish history, remained a dream. In a dream or fantasy, everything is perfect, utopian, serene and smooth. In the challenging world of reality, nation building is a complicated, painful and oftentimes fractious struggle. The eternal Land of Israel — as the home of universally knowledgeable, Torah-observant Jews, where all will thirst for the Word of God — remains the dream, the standard, the hoped-for better world that will undoubtedly yet arrive.

The State of Israel remains in the current reality a work in progress. It is part of an imperfect and dangerous world, and it is comprised of fallible human beings. Nevertheless, most Jews believe that the State of Israel has to somehow aspire to achieve the holiness and positive worldwide influence that the concept of a Jewish state implies. Jews understand that the State of Israel is held to more rigid standards of decency and morality than its other national counterparts. Yet, it is essential that the State of Israel be encouraged and not only criticized, uplifted and not always demeaned, valued and appreciated and not merely taken for granted.

The Holy Land remains holy for all of mankind. It is the Jews who have kept it in trust for the benefit and well being of all faiths and peoples since the time of Abraham. Though it is the particular and eternal homeland of the Jewish People, we are always aware of the words of the prophet Isaiah, "For My house shall be a house of prayer for all nations." May that day come soon.

Index

A

Aaron   19, 20, 156
Abba, Rav   89
Abel   288
abortion   14, 15, 16, 83, 86, 89, 129
Abraham   217, 223, 230, 231, 263, 288, 294, 295, 296,
Achashverus   165
Adam   47, 53, 134, 287
afikoman   184
Aharon   19
Akiva, Rabbi   97, 143, 187, 190, 204
Aleinu   89
Alexander Janneus   157
aliyah   151, 152
Alsace   187
Amalekites   286
America (United States)   93, 101, 131
Amidah   84, 86, 89, 90, 94
Amos   260
Amsterdam   270
anti-semitism   165, 206, 208, 231, 247, 291, 292
Arvit (see Maariv)   88
Ashbili, Rabbi Yom Tov ben Avraham ibn (Ritva)   181
Ashkenazi (Ari), Rabbi Isaac Luria   111
Ashkenazi, Rabbi Zvi   270
Ashkenazic customs   23, 29, 91, 95, 111, 180, 181, 203, 247
Ashkenazim   29
Avot (Ethics of the Fathers)   250
Azulai, Rabbi Chaim Yosef David   264

B

baal tashchit   275, 276
Baalei tefillah (masters of prayer)   92
Babylonia   125, 159, 228, 230, 202, 205, 267
Babylonian exile   125, 160
badchan   30
Bais Yaakov   234
Bar Kokhba   186, 190
Bar Kokhba, Shimon   187, 205
Bar Mitzvah   22, 23, 24, 25, 26, 27, 73, 75

Bar Rokba   202
Bat Mitzvah   22, 23, 24
Batei midrash (study halls)   192
ben David, Mordechai   268
Benjamin of Tudela   264, 265
Berlin, Rabbi Naftali Zvi Yehudah   111
Bible   16, 23, 34, 35, 41, 54, 81, 83, 105, 110, 125, 135, 136, 138, 160, 193, 225, 214, 220, 224, 241, 255, 257, 258, 260, 278, 287, 288, 293, 296
bikurim   195
Birchot nisuim   29
birth   13, 14, 15
blintzes   196
Blois   208, 209
blood libel   208, 291, 292
Boaz   110
Bolshevik Revolution   206
Book of Esther   162, 166, 284
Book of Lamentations/Eichah   203, 207, 267
Book of Ruth   193
Brit   17, 200
Bruriah   23
Byelorussia   206
Byzantine Christian   231, 269

C

Cain   288
cantor, cantors (*chazan*)   91, 93, 267
Cantor, Eddie   92
Carlebach, Shlomo   268
Central Europe   151, 180, 206, 264
Chafetz Chaim   215
Chagall, Marc   271
Chagy, Berele   92
challah   23, 24, 104, 108
chametz   122, 171, 172, 173, 178, 180, 181, 256
Chanukah   119, 153, 154, 155, 157, 205, 270, 284, 285
charity   59, 63, 216
charoset   184, 185
Chassidic customs   248, 72, 111, 178
Chassidic movement   253
Chassidut   247
Chattan Bereshit   151

Ritual slaughterer (*shochet*)   65
Romans, Rome   157, 159, 186, 187, 190, 197, 198, 199, 202, 203, 205, 231, 261, 262, 267, 269, 273
Rosenblatt, Yossele   92
Rosh Chodesh   123, 284
Rosh Hashanah   89, 119, 124, 125, 127, 128, 129, 130, 131, 133, 134, 135, 137, 138, 139, 145, 159, 168, 284
Russia   99, 206
Ruth   23, 110

S

Saadya Gaon, Rabbi   238
Sabbath of Repentance (see Shabbath Shuvah)   139
Sabbath songs   267
Sabbath *zemirot*   203
Sabbath   15, 16, 17, 19, 23, 26, 39, 59, 74, 83, 99, 102, 104, 105, 106, 107, 109, 110, 111, 112, 113, 114, 116, 117, 119, 122, 139, 143, 145, 148, 160, 161, 170, 200, 202, 203, 218, 247, 261, 266, 296
Sabin, Leonard   282
Sadducees (Tzadokim)   157
Salk, Jonas   282
sandak   18
Sanhedrin   169
Sarah   16, 217, 223, 263
Sassportas, Rabbi Jacob   270
Schnirer, Sarah   234
Sea of Galilee   95
Seder   178, 183, 184, 185, 256, 291, 297
Sefirah   186, 187, 188, 189, 190
Sephardic customs   23, 29, 38, 91, 94, 111, 181, 203, 247
Sephardim   29
Septuagint   160
Seventeenth of Tamuz   197, 198, 199
sexual relations   51, 207, 244
sexuality   50, 244, 245
Shabbat Chazon   202, 203
Shabbat Hagadol   139, 140
Shabbat Shuvah   139, 140, 141
Shabbat   *see* Sabbath
Shach, Rabbi Elazar Menachem Mann   31
Shacharit   83, 86, 87, 88, 89
shadchanim (matchmakers)   48

Shalom bayit   105
Shalom Zachor   15
Shavuot   119, 145, 150, 186, 188, 189, 190, 192, 193, 194, 195, 196, 284
shechitah   279
Shehechiyanu   200
Shema Yisrael   77, 84, 86, 88, 90, 122
Sheva Brachot   29, 49
shidduch system   48
Shimon bar Yochai, Rabbi   190, 253
Shimon   154, 156, 157
Shiva   32, 217
Shmini Atzeret   95, 150, 284
shofar   128, 129
shtieblach   229
shtreimel   111, 248, 246
Shushan   162, 163, 166
Siddur   233
Simchat Torah   150, 151, 152
Sinai Desert   114, 145, 255
Sinai   66, 75, 76, 84, 108, 113, 124, 134, 161, 169, 190, 194, 195, 234, 237, 240, 255
skullcap (*yarmulke, kippah*)   142, 246, 247
Soloveitchik, Rabbi Chaim   250
Song of Songs   134
South Africa   93
South America   93
Spain   144, 181, 228, 264
Spanish Expulsion   202, 206
Speyer   187, 210
Stalin, Joseph   64, 146, 231
Succah   146
Succot   94, 95, 119, 125, 135, 145, 146, 147, 149, 150, 284, 288
Sudar   247
synagogue   15, 17, 39, 42, 92, 97, 102, 105, 119, 139, 162, 166, 196, 202, 203, 207, 218, 261, 265
Syria   291

T

Tabernacle   114, 124
Tachanun   84
Taharat hamishpachah (family purity)   51
tallit gadol   71, 73
tallit katan   72
tallit   71, 83, 149, 151